CAN'T KEEP
A STRAIGHT FACE

A lesbian looks and laughs at life

by
ELLEN ORLEANS

illustrated by
NOREEN STEVENS

Laugh Lines Press

This project funded in part by grants from the Boulder Arts
Commission, an agency of the Boulder City Council,
and by the Boulder Queer Collective.

Audre Lorde quotation from "The Transformation of Silence into
Language and Action" by Audre Lorde, as published in *Sister
Outsider*, © Crossing Press, P.O. Box 1048, Freedom, CA 95019.
Used by permission.

"All Day Always" by Deidre McCalla, © 1987 Chetwood Arts
Music. Lyrics printed by permission. All rights reserved.

"Lay Me Down" from *Walk That Edge* © 1987 Heather Bishop
(SOCAN). Lyrics printed by permission.

Every effort has been made to locate copyright owners and to
secure permissions for material used in this book.

For information contact Rosalind Warren, Laugh Lines Press,
P.O. Box 259, Bala Cynwyd, PA 19004 215-668-4252

Cover and interior illustrations by Noreen Stevens
Author's photograph © Kate Hershenson
Interior design by Ellen Orleans
Printed in U.S.A.

Library of Congress Catalog Card Number 93-77286

Can't keep a straight face: a lesbian looks and laughs at life
p. cm
ISBN 0-9632526-1-5
1. Lesbians–Humor
2. Humor–Gay/Lesbian life
3. Feminist/Lesbian Studies–humor
4. Women–humor

I. Ellen Orleans, 1961–

For Lori,
who encouraged me
with her laughter

HUMOR=LIFE

CONTENTS

FOREWORD

I collected the essays for *Can't Keep A Straight Face* from three years' worth of my work, most of which first appeared in a monthly column I write for Denver's *Quest* magazine.

As I pulled these essays together for national publication, I was faced with the question of how to present them. (I acknowledge that this isn't the most earth-shattering problem in the world, easily surpassed—for example—by toxic waste, TV violence and internalized homophobia.)

Still, I wondered if I should organize them somehow. Should I lump them together by theme, tone or style? Group them into sections: i.e., heavy vs. fluff, personal vs. political? (Oops. How embarrassing of me to forget that the personal *is* political.)

In the end though, I left them pretty much in the order in which I wrote them. Yes, I was tempted to update certain pieces. For example, when I wrote "Turning On and Tuning In" back in 1989, local gossip hadn't yet established Melissa Etheridge as a lesbian. With that piece of speculation now intact, we no longer have to wonder "is she or isn't she?" But instead of substituting yet another, still ambiguous, performer, I left Melissa there, letting that essay reflect its time.

As a people, our queer family has endured—and still faces— so much pain and violence. Here in Colorado, a message of hate and fear was driven home this November, when voters passed Amendment 2, a law that takes away civil rights for lesbians, gay men and bisexuals. Under this law, it's legal to fire employees because they're queer; it's legal for landlords to say, "I don't rent to lesbians."

Add to this law the gay-bashings, the battles for child custody, the gay teen suicide rate, the deaths from breast cancer and AIDS, and suddenly an inner voice asks, "What could possibly be funny about being a lesbian? Wouldn't a brooding diatribe on heterosexist oppression be more to the point?"

But I choose humor because laughter breaks down barriers. Laughter cuts through the stereotypes; it gives us a break from the all-too-real heterosexist oppression out there. But mostly, humor gives us hope: hope for a better future for all of us.

It's my hope, then, that these essays will not only bring a smile to your face, but also strength to your spirit.

> Ellen Orleans
> Boulder, Colorado
> December 1992

My silences had not protected me. Your silence will not protect you.
Audre Lorde, 1934-1992

CAN'T KEEP A STRAIGHT FACE

JUST A PHONE CALL AWAY

I spent Thanksgiving on the East Coast with Lori, my GLP. That's "girlfriend/lover/partner" to those of you not up on the latest of lesbian slang. (Which probably includes all of you, since I just made up the term.) We were visiting my relatives, and by the fifth day, we were suffering from an acute attack of lesbian withdrawal.

"You know," I said to Lori, "We need support for travelers and other isolated lesbians. We need "Dial-a-Dyke.""

Think about it. All those times you've needed a quick fix of lesbian culture. Like the summer you were camping at Mesa Verde, surrounded by heterosexual families, and about to kill the man two campsites down who'd hooked up a television and VCR. Or back in '87, at your family reunion, when your aunt Madeline asked you for the sixth time, "So, when are you moving back home?"

Yup, Dial-a-Dyke is what we need, and I've even figured out the particulars. Here's how it works.

Instead of enduring a prolonged bout of irritability or succumbing to an explosive rage, I merely excuse myself, dash to the nearest telephone and call the 800 number. (The cost is picked up by the National Endowment for the Arts. Don't scoff. This is *my* fantasy, and *I* say it's a toll-free call.)

Okay, so I dial 1-800-LES-BIAN. Easy enough. Music plays, a voice sings, "There is a reason we gather here." It's Deidre McCalla. I feel myself beginning to loosen up.

A new voice comes on. "Hi. You've reached the Lesbian Line, your 'Homo Away from Home.' I'm Robin Tyler and for the next half hour, you'll be receiving a lifesaving infusion of lesbianism. So, sit back, relax—you're among friends."

A pause, then new music in the background. "Bonjour, this is Lucie Blue. I'd like to sing for you now a new song off my album which is new also. I've trained my dog to whistle, so she'll be singing too." They sing for a while, then. . .

"Greetings! I'm Professor Lillian Coswell, Ph. D., and it's time for Lesbian Literature. First a little trivia. Did you know that Willa Cather was a lesbian? Bet they didn't teach you that in high school. That Virginia Woolf and Edna St. Vincent Millay had female lovers? Now, two poems by Paula Gunn Allen. . ."

Then Robin's back and plays a Dolly Parton and Melissa Etheridge duet, from the "If they Aren't, They Oughta Be" album.

After that, it's Joanne Loulan. "Hi. How are you doing? Nice haircut. Excuse me, but do you have a moment? I'd like to talk about your vagina. Not actually your vagina in particular, but women's vaginas in general. . . "

Next up, it's Katherine Forrest, who reads a sex scene from her latest detective mystery. Then Meg Christian's recording of "Leaping Lesbians" pulls me out of the fantasy I'd drifted into while listening to Ms. Forrest. By now I'm smiling widely as I hear. . .

"Thanks for coming out! This is Kate Clinton. Think about this—which came first, the tampon or the egg?"

A commanding voice follows. "Hello. This is Ginny Apuzzo, from the GLLGPCISNTF. For those of you who haven't kept up with initials, that's the Gay and Lesbian—Let's Get Political,

C'mon I'm Serious—National Task Force. Here's an update on lesbian news throughout the world. . . "

"Well, hello. Robin here again. That just about winds up this month's lesbian line. Coming next month, k.d. lang and Phranc sing 'I Think Your Crew Cut's Swell.' I myself will attempt to channel Eleanor Roosevelt. Oh, by the way, this isn't really an 800 number. You'll be billed 36 bucks for this call. Just kidding!"

"We're going to finish up now with a rendition of Margie Adam's *We Shall Go Forth*, sung by the Denver Women's Chorus. Enjoy it, and go forth, renewed by lesbian energy."

As the music surges, then softens, I do indeed feel refreshed. Then Robin announces: "This concludes the Lesbian Line for this month. To obtain information about lesbian events in your area, press 1. To talk with a counselor, press 2. To order cassettes or CD's of any of this month's performers, press 3. To increase your orgasmic response, press 4."

I bet she's just kidding. But just in case. . .

TURNING ON AND TUNING IN

Some people are waiting for the Second Coming. Others look eagerly to the Dawn of the New Age. Me? I'm waiting for a lesbian TV station.

That's right. I want to see lipstick lesbians strutting on soaps, dyke detectives gunning down crooked judges, lesbian rugby teams appearing on our own version of "Wheel of Fortune." But more than all this, I want to see lesbian commercials. Yes, I believe I would actually start watching TV again just to see us queer gals between the programs.

Imagine this scene for AT&T: An older, grey-haired couple sits quietly by a fire. She is reading a book, he leafs through the paper. The grandfather clock strikes 10 pm. The phone rings. She gets up to answer it and calls to him excitedly, "Oh, George. It's Ellie and Melanie calling from Boston."

Eagerly he rises from his chair and stands by her side. "The new place is working out? That's great. Uh, huh." She turns to her husband, and reports, "They got the sheets and down comforter we sent," then returns her attention the receiver. "Melanie's co-dependency group is going well. I'm so glad. Did you get to the Pride Parade? We read about it in the paper. What?

You did? Congratulations!" Again she conveys the news, "George, Ellie got the position at the Safehouse. " Back to the receiver: "Hold on, Dad wants to say hello."

Just warms your heart, doesn't it? Or picture this:

A woman stands in front of a beautiful island resort and asks the viewer, *Do you know me? For centuries, my life and writings have influenced millions. But when I want to reserve a room for a night, do they recognize me? Not a chance. That's why whenever I travel to the Greek Isles, I carry the American Express Card.* A big American Express Card appears on the screen, the letters S-A-P-P-H-O stamped across it.

Of course, not all commercials will be in good taste. We're bound to have to tolerate some crassness. Like the ad for Duracell batteries. The camera pans in on a half-dozen vibrators of various colors and shapes, all buzzing and wriggling. A female voiceover announces, "Can you guess which vibrator has Duracell-brand batteries?" A time lapse of 6-1/2 hours is simulated and we see that only the pink pearl-diver vibrator is still pulsating away. The voice continues; "That's right. Duracell lasts up to two-and-a-half times longer than conventional batteries. For pleasure you can count on, it's Duracell."

Or imagine it's Saturday night. You've come home early from a discouraging date with Abigail, an elusive woman on whom you have a heavy crush. She's just told you that she needs to devote herself entirely to her thesis on *Global Warming and Its Effect on the Circulatory Systems of North Atlantic Shellfish* and therefore doesn't have time to spend with you.

Dejected, you plop yourself in front of the tube, flip to K-LES, and watch a rerun of the lesbian remake of *Oklahoma!* (now entitled *Oklahomosexual!*, of course). As you drift off, the voice of Teresa Trull jumps out across your living room, *I'd like to make love with you. . .*

"Yes," a booming voice announces, "KTEL Records is proud to offer this very special package of lesbian love songs. Remember this one?" In the background, you hear Holly Near, who invitingly urges you not to hold back.

Yes, you'll be dancing in the moonlight to the sounds of Margie Adam, Kay Gardner and Lucie Blue. Imagine getting cozy in front of the fire with a special friend as Heather Bishop sings right to you. . . Overdub of Heather Bishop, *Take me now, take me in your arms and lay me down, lay me down slow. . .*" That's right, these are the original recordings of the original artists, before they decided to go mainstream and use ambiguous gender terminology.

This very special three-album collection can be yours for only $19.95. You heard it right, just $19.95—but that's not all! If you order now, you'll also receive *Are They or Aren't They*—a unique collection of songs from women we've always wondered about. Joan Armatrading, Melissa Etheridge, Dolly Parton and more. Yes, that's right, *Are They or Aren't They* is yours absolutely free when you order now. Unbelievable, isn't it? But wait, there's more.

If you place your call in the next 24 hours, you'll get a very special gift from us. A one-of-a-kind sound recording, entitled "Tracy Comes Out" a collection of lesbian songs written and performed by Tracy Chapman. It's the album you've been hoping for from Tracy. Operators are standing by. To order by phone, call. . .

Your phone rings. It's Abigail. "I'm sorry to call so late," she says, "but I was watching a late movie, and this commercial for lesbian love songs came on and I started thinking about us, and maybe. . . I'd like to give it another chance."

Lesbian television. It will be worth the wait.

Coming up next.... Kate + Allie, the unedited tapes

MAKING HOMOPHOBIA WORK FOR YOU

We live in an imperfect world. Homophobia, heterosexism, anti-gay hatred. No matter what you call it, it stinks. But as long as it's with us (and let's keep working to eradicate it), it's time to take a creative view of the situation. It's time to make homophobia work for you.

"What?" you say. "Work for me? How can I do that?"

Well, let me tell you—I've heard stories from some pretty ingenious folks out there. Consider, for example, my friends Penelope and Matilda (not their real names). They received one of those overnight offers from a condo company. The situation goes like this: A real estate developer, Overkill International (not its real name) invites you to stay at their fancy-schmancy resort for two nights. You eat free meals, soak in the hot springs, hike around the mountains—you even get $50 for expenses.

The catch? You have to listen to a two-hour, hard-sell sales pitch about investing in the company's time-sharing vacation condominiums. For heterosexual couples, both the husband and wife have to attend. For lesbian couples? Hey, in the eyes of Overkill International, we don't exist. So, even though Penelope and Matilda have been together for six years, only

19

Matilda had to endure the high-pressure pitch, while Penelope got to lounge around and read the latest Stoner McTavish mystery. What a deal.

Have you heard about the two enterprising gay men in upstate New York? Seems there was a convention there, and these guys were on their way to a workshop. As they were walking along, who do they chance to meet but a bunch of self-righteous right-wingers, protesting outside a women's health clinic. The men wanted to do something, but felt logical discussion or mere yelling would do no good. Then one of them received divine inspiration. He kissed his boyfriend. His boyfriend kissed him back. And they kept kissing and hugging, right in front of the group.

Well, this was just too much for the protesters. Offensive language, screaming contests—they just "prayed" louder. But love? Men loving each other?

The protesters' kids started tugging on their parents' sleeves. "Daddy, why is that man kissing another man?"

"Not now, Junior," they said, looking at each other. What to do? Yell out "faggots"? The men only smiled back. Go push 'em around? They weren't supposed to be violent. Gently move them apart? Not a chance. Hell, that would mean touching them and then the protesters' buddies might think that they were queer too.

The men continued kissing. The protesters got antsy. The mothers didn't want their kids to see this, the men didn't want their wives to see it. Confused and anxious, the anti-choice people packed up and left.

And from personal experience, I give this account: A couple of years ago, my partner Lori and I (our real names) were up near Aspen. The inn in which we were staying had a pool and small hot tub. We were hoping to catch a romantic half-hour in the tub, so we put on our swimsuits and wandered on over. Disappointed to see a man and woman sitting in the tub, we decided to play in the pool first. We did silly lesbian lovers' stuff: Lori pulled me in circles, I pretended I was a shark and dove down to bite her toes. I carried her, she carried me, and then we were cold, so—privacy or no privacy—we headed to the hot tub.

Smiling politely, we sat down opposite the two. The woman returned my smile with a transparent one of her own, then looked at her watch. "My, it's gotten so late," she exclaimed.

"Yes, we really need to get ready for dinner," the man replied. Within seconds, they were gone. The tub was ours. . .

SEMANTICALLY SPEAKING

Some female homosexuals use the term "gay woman" to describe themselves, others prefer "lesbian." Which is the right word for you?

Well, "gay" *is* a simpler word. It has fewer syllables than lesbian and sounds festive, while lesbian has a no-nonsense "roll up the shirt sleeves and get down to business" feel about it.

Also, lesbian is both a noun and an adjective, and therefore confusing. We talk about lesbian culture, lesbian music and lesbian sex, but to speak of a "lesbian woman" is apparently redundant. Instead she is simply a lesbian which means she is defined by a noun instead of an adjective and you can imagine the political implications of that.

The other thing about "lesbian" is that it's tricky to type. C'mon, 'fess up, how many times have you inadvertently typed "lesbain" or "lesbina" while knocking out a press release?

By the way, "lesbain" is an ancient Sapphic curse. It is cast upon women who, when you tell them you're queer, haughtily reply, "I refuse to limit myself with labels."

And what is a "lesbina"? A lesbian ballerina. Of course.

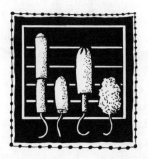

LESBIAN PREFERENCES

Tampons. Kate Clinton started her career around them (figuratively speaking) and since they were such an auspicious beginning for her, I'd like to share some of my thoughts on the matter. First of all: what brand do lesbians prefer most? Has anyone done a woman-on-the-street survey of this? Not that I'd heard of, so I decided to do my own.

First stop, Crystal Market in Boulder. I stopped a woman wearing an Indian print skirt, T'ai Chi shoes and a "Heal the Earth" T-shirt.

"Excuse me," I asked, "are you a lesbian?"

"No," she smiled, "but thanks for asking."

Reddening profusely, I was saved by the woman behind her who piped up, "I am. What can I do for you?"

"I'm researching tampon use, and—"

"Sorry," she said, "They give me cramps. I use pads."

I turned to the next woman exiting the store. She was wearing baggy shorts, beat-up Reeboks and a shirt that said, "I Saw You Naked at Michigan."

"Pardon me, " I asked, "I'm doing a survey on lesbians and tampons. Are you a dyke, by any chance? "

"Of course," she said, looking at me as if I were nuts.

"What brand of tampons do you prefer?"

"Don't use them, she said, pulling a small bag of menstrual sponges out of her grocery bag. "I use these. They're reusable and don't aid the patriarchy's misogynist commercial exploitation of the female species."

Though thoroughly frustrated in my research, I thanked her and recalled my first and last experience with menstrual sponges. I had just purchased my first set, and had dropped them in a pan of boiling water to be sterilized. The phone rang and I went to answer it. It was a friend I hadn't talked to in weeks, and we got into a conversation about camping trips and ex-lovers. Toward the end of the conversation, I smelled something a little odd, but knew I wasn't cooking any food, so let it go. A few minutes later I wandered into the kitchen and there, on the stove, sat a burned-out pan, boiled dry with nothing but a little sticky goo where the sponges had been. Needless to say, I wasn't converted.

Anyway, back to my research. The next weekend I trotted down to the Book Garden in Denver. I approached a woman with wire-frame glasses, a Sweet Honey in the Rock T-shirt and a copy of *Wildfire*. Her choice (not Sonia Johnson's, but the woman I was interviewing) was Tampax brand, because that's what her mother used, and she believed in honoring the matriarchy. "But I never use the kind with plastic petal-leaf inserters." She told me, "Ecologically incorrect. Very ecologically incorrect."

My next group was a bunch of dykes just finishing up a soccer match on their way to a Two Nice Girls concert. "OB's," they told me, almost unanimously. "They're small, you can stick them in the pocket of your 501's and no one knows they're there. Great for anyone who wouldn't be caught dead with a purse."

All this tampon research reminded me of a housemate I had several years back. We'd just moved into an old house, and early on had trouble with the toilet being stopped up.

Wrestling with the plunger she grumbled, "I just hope there aren't any tampons clogging it up. Anyone who flushes tampons down toilets should be shot."

"Shot?" I thought, "Isn't that just a little extreme?"

Imagine it. A firing squad lined up, the prisoners, blindfolded, standing against the wall. Their crimes are read out loud: international terrorism, kidnapping and extortion, hijacking military aircraft, flushing tampons down the toilet.

The firing squad would all put down their rifles, scratch their heads, and mutter to each other, "Gee, I don't know much about tampons. Sure, clogged toilets are a nuisance, but this sure seems like overreacting."

For reasons of demographic accuracy, I tried to interview older lesbians, but I get shy around lesbians ten or more years older than me, especially when asking them about tampon choices, so that didn't work very well.

Eventually, my research stalled and I never did get any solid results. But I am on to bigger and better things now. We lesbians constitute a huge, untapped consumer market. Yes, someday in the not-so-distant future, I'll be walking in a shopping mall and will accidentally make eye contact with one of those ubiquitous market research people. "Excuse me," the market research person will say, " We are doing research on the brand of pet food lesbians most prefer for their cats. Do you have a cat?"

"Well, yes." I'll answer.

"Great. And are you a lesbian?"

"I certainly am. And thanks for asking."

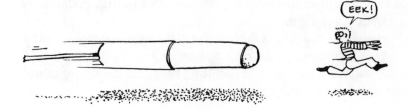

LETTING THE BUYER BEWARE

I see now that they're putting warning labels on alcohol, similar to the kind on cigarette packs. This time, I hope they don't mess around for twenty years before they come up with effective wording.

Remember how cigarettes started out? WARNING: *The Surgeon General has determined that smoking may be hazardous to your health.* Then it got bold and changed to "smoking *is* hazardous to your health." Finally, it actually got specific, with warnings of underweight fetuses, emphysema, and premature death.

But is any of this really effective? Can such tactics make even a dent against the billion-dollar-a-year tobacco industry? I think not. Let us then, instead explore some novel approaches to this problem.

WARNING: *Getting hooked on these will cause you to be a social outcast at Central American benefits, lesbian separatist potlucks and domestic plane flights.*

WARNING: *You'll miss the best part of the movie when you run out of the theater to satisfy your nicotine cravings.*

WARNING: *Once you start smoking these, the number of women available for dates will be reduced by 54%.*

Yes, it's the social, not medical, angle that gets the message across.

The same holds true in the case of alcohol. Consider this scenario: You are at a party without your lover, who is home with a sore throat. You're about to crack open your third beer, when you happen to glance at the print on the side of the can:

WARNING: *Drinking too much of this stuff may cause impairment to your rational thinking and you might end up in bed with that hot lesbian you've been staring at all night and then the next day your 6-year committed, monogamous relationship is going to be on the skids, and you just bought a house together, and gosh are you ever going to be sorry!*

But why stop with alcohol and cigarettes? How about a big sign in front of Target or K-Mart? WARNING: *Entering this store may cause you to spend ungodly sums on assorted plastic items for which you have neither need nor space.*

On frozen dinners. WARNING: *The photograph on the outside of this box improperly suggests that the entree within is both tasty and nutritious. Don't count on it.*

On skin-tight leather pants. WARNING: *Wearing of this garment may result in the attraction of unfamiliar women and the likelihood of them running their hands up and down your thighs. But hey, isn't that what you were hoping for in the first place?*

On Naiad romances. WARNING: *Reading this book may cause you to form unrealistic beliefs about sex. Specifically, you'll likely develop the misconception that lesbian sex is heavenly and flawless every time and that you'll always have an orgasm (and probably multiple orgasms), especially if it's the first time and neither of you have ever slept with a woman before.*

Or perhaps, just perhaps, with advanced merchandising techniques, our warning labels could become buyer-specific. I can imagine this one on a Prelude vibrator: WARNING TO STRAIGHT WOMEN: *Application of this item in certain areas can cause extreme pleasure and raise doubts as to the need for men in your life.*

Don't say we didn't warn you.

A TALE OF TWO KITTIES

Part One

Ah, the staying power of the almighty feline beast. . . I've known women who, in a single decade, have gone through four jobs, six apartments and three lovers, but still have the same cat.

Therefore, I regarded it as an auspicious sign when Isis—my lover's cat—took a liking to me early on. In fact, I remember a long telephone conversation with my friend Carol just as Lori and I were beginning to date. Carol and I were discussing whether my new situation with Lori was a capital "R" or small "r" relationship.

As we talked, I was sewing a catnip mouse. At one point I asked, "Can you hold on a minute? I need to get more thread."

"What are you sewing?" Carol asked.

"A toy mouse for Lori's cat."

"By hand?" she asked, incredulous.

"Yeah. I've finished the tail and ears, now I'm sewing on individual whiskers."

"Well, Ellen," she said, "you may not be ready to hear this, but I'll tell you anyway. Sewing a toy mouse to please a woman's cat is a sure sign that you are in capital 'R' relationship. In fact, you might even be in love."

She was right, of course, and eight months later Lori and I (and Isis) moved in together. My love for Isis, however, quickly became strained. You see, Isis developed an annoying habit of walking up to my desk (I work at home) and meowing loudly. From there the scenario goes like this:

I get up, walk to the front door and ask, "Do you need out?"
"Meow!"
(She won't go out the door.)
Do you need food?
"Meow!"
(The food bowl is full.)
Is the litter box blocked off?
"Meow!"
(No, it's fully accessible.)
"Do you want to play in the garage?"
"Meow!"
(She doesn't budge.)
"Do you want to be held?" I try picking her up but with a militant "Rrrr!," she rappels off my chest.

You'd think I'd just scoop her up and put her outdoors. Well, our house has a little problem. Halfway up the outside walls, right below the windows, there's a brick ledge that runs around the house. A narrow ledge, it's just wide enough for a small four-legged creature.

What this means is that no matter what we're doing in the house—washing dishes, talking long-distance, meditating, or making love—Isis can walk up to any window and meow, noisily and insistently and continually, until one of us lets her in.

For a while, Isis slept during the day: all was peaceful and I was able to work. But then, around 10 pm she'd become active and spend the night jumping from my dresser to the window sill and back. Alternatively, she'd walk on my head.

At such times, both Lori and I seriously wondered how this cat could possibly be named Isis, after the Egyptian Mother

Goddess. For surely when your cat meows to go out at 2 am, then back in again at 4 am, it takes great acts of searching to find any sign of the revered, the holy, or the sacred in the creature.

Part Two

She was grey and had no name. She spent her first two days pressing herself into a corner. She was our new cat.

Her mission? To be a companion and playmate for Isis, and thus end Isis's ever-present meowing, which we believed was brought on by her long hours of tedium and boredom.

Lesson One: Don't ever give a cat a mission.

By day, the grey cat hid behind the couch, avoiding Isis's snarls. At night Isis paced the bed—on guard duty—while the grey cat, lying just outside the bedroom door, periodically sent out pitiful meows.

Eventually, the situation improved. Sort of. Instead of hiding, the new cat began snarling back. Whenever the two encountered each other, Isis screamed at the top of her kitty lungs, then dashed madly off. Judging by the fracas, I expected to see tufts of fur and pools of blood after one of these battles. But neither cat was ever hurt. Just lots of noise.

I thought, "Hey! A new model for our military policy. Put only blanks in our nuclear warheads and Trident missiles. Make as loud a racket as you like, but no death or destruction allowed."

Meanwhile, tired of calling the grey cat, "the grey cat," Lori and I were enmeshed in the game of "name-the-cat." Obvious choices like Misty and Smoky seemed trite. We considered exotic names like Ananda—which means absolute bliss—hoping she'd take the hint, but she was a down-to-earth sort of cat. However, the name "Amanda" (which is darn close to Ananda) kept resurfacing. Sounding solid and grounded, it fit this cat. So "Amanda" it was.

Lesson Two: Just because you settle on a cat's name doesn't mean that the cat agrees with you.

Having established her new name, we tried calling her in

from the yard. "Amanda," we called, "here, Amanda!" No dice.

"Here kitty, kitty, " we tried. Instantly she appeared on the doorstep. So she became (unofficially) Amanda Kitty, Kitty.

We later read that "Amanda" was the fifth most popular name for new babies in Boulder County. We were proud to have reached—in our small way—trendiness.

Like a lot of lesbians, I occasionally discover life's greater truths by way of a cat. (It's cheaper than therapy.) One cold morning, Isis was meowing to be let out into the backyard through the sliding glass door. However, the frozen condensation on the door had sealed it shut.

Instead, I opened the front door. "Come on, Isis," I called, "Come out the front door, it goes outside too." She wasn't interested.

"Isis," I insisted, "You can get to the backyard from the front. It's all attached."

Finally she moved towards the front door and leapt out.

Closing it behind me, I muttered, "What a weird cat." But as I thought about it, I realized that I do the same thing. I get stuck thinking there is only one way out. Really, though, my "backyard"—the place where dreams and adventure lie—can be reached through not one, but many, doors. And as I step out, you can bet that I'll have a cat along, showing me the way.

A DYKE BY ANY OTHER NAME

One day last summer I was hanging out at the ball fields, when my friend Karin showed up and introduced me to two of her friends, Bev and Billie. As we all sat in the bleachers, checking out the scene, Bev remarked, "There's Leona."

"How do you know her?" I asked.

"Oh, she goes to the same church we do," Billie replied. I looked at Billie and Bev; they didn't look like church-going types to me, but hey, you can't tell by looking.

"What church do you go to?" I asked.

Billie gave me a weird look. Her lover intervened. "She means, dear, that Leona is a PLU."

"What's that stand for? Political Lesbian Underground?"

"Person Like Us," Karin told me, amazed at my denseness, "get it?"

I didn't.

"Dyke, Ellen. She's a dyke."

"Oh."

Maybe I came out at the wrong time, or maybe I hang out with an unimaginative crowd, but I call a lesbian a lesbian (unless I call her a dyke). The other exception is when I'm talking to my aunt and use the genteel "gay."

After the incident at the ball field, I began asking women about the code words they use.

"Family," a popular term, is one I often hear from my friend Rita. I remember once, when Rita was telling me about a co-worker, she leaned over and whispered confidentially, "then I find out she's family!"

"Rita," I wanted to say, "We're at an Alix Dobkin concert, for god's sake. You can say 'lesbian'."

Perhaps I'm missing the point. Maybe women prefer code words because of the nuances they convey. "Family" does suggest feelings of togetherness that "lesbian" does not. Also, as I continue exploring the realm of code words, I've discovered that this secret language is not only descriptive, but admittedly kinda cool.

The phrase "a family resemblance" is used to comment on an unknown woman. For example, Joan and Tara are at Alfalfa's deli, watching a counter clerk. Joan says, "I see a certain 'family resemblance,' don't you?"

"If not," Tara replies, "at least a DIT (Dyke In Training)."

While I'm not sure of the precise difference between a DIT and another term, "Lesbian Wannabe," I think it has to do with intention. Lesbian Wannabe's are straight women who get into the lesbian culture because it's in vogue. DIT's are on the verge of coming out (whether they know it or not), and are sincere in their desire to join the lesbian world.

Many code words are merely shorthand, used when playing Spot-the-Dyke. To see how it works, let's listen to Sarah and Rivka as they walk the mall.

They both look at the same woman, then at each other. Sarah asks, "What do you think?"

Rivka knows Sarah isn't asking if she thinks the women perms her hair, has kids, or sells insurance for a living. It's clear that "What do you think?" means "Do you think she's a dyke?"

Sometimes it hardly takes any words at all.

"DOR" (Dyke on the Right).

"Yeah and DOL too."

"There's one."

"Yup."

"The woman in the hightops. Don't you think so?"

"Definitely."

Some women call out "d-alert!" Others use "gay-dar," sounding "beep, beep" when they pass a lesbian. One group of friends developed an intricate system of zaps and zots. Dykes were zaps; straights were zots. If you brought a straight women out, you had "zapped a zot."

Another colorful expression, "member of the committee," is one of my favorites. I imagine a diverse collection of dykes sitting around a long table, making earth-shattering decisions.

Picture it. A straight friend comes up and says, "I just heard that the government is slashing military funding and using the money to shelter homeless people, give out free AZT, and build recycling plants. How did that all happen?"

"Well," you say, shrugging your shoulders, "A bunch of us 'members of the committee' got together and said, 'Let's do it'."

"Wow, I never knew you wielded such power."

"Yes, it's one of the awesome responsibilities of being a 'member of the committee.' By the way, tomorrow we exile Donald Wildmon *and* solve the environmental crisis."

Another wonderful word for lesbians is "advanced," as in "not only is she an excellent lawyer and sculptor, but she's also *advanced*." Advanced—it gives me a rush just to *say* it.

Two of the more unusual terms I've heard for lesbians are "Bulgarians" and "Lobos." "Lobo," the Spanish word for "wolf," is a term used in the Los Angeles area. Of course, I got this information from a straight woman who is a bit of a Lesbian Wannabe, so it could have no factual basis whatsoever.

Still I like the expression and the images it conjures up. I can envision a report on the 6 o'clock news: "Today a group of right-wing fundamentalists tried to block a women's health clinic.

They were thwarted in their attempt by a large pack of lobos, who wandered in from the foothills."

Now that's one to set off your gaydar-radar—Beep, beep, zap, zap.

THE ENVIRONMENTAL SHOPPER

Whoever said that the personal is political wasn't kidding. It was one of those warm March days. I was sitting outside on a chaise lounge, daydreaming in the afternoon sun. . .

I'm on a beach on an idyllic tropical island, thousands of miles away from civilization and the monotonous grind of daily living in the post-Industrial Age. In the clear blue sea in front of me, I see a lesbian mermaid. She calls out my name and beckons me to her.

We dive through the waves together, laughing and playing in the warm ocean water. I am enchanted by the droplets of water clinging to her skin, enthralled by her sleek, effortless movements and entranced by her deep violet eyes.

She takes my hand and says, "Follow me." We go to the shore, where she transforms into a human. Beneath the warm rays of the sun, she gently strokes my cheek. My body pulsates. Then, out of the corner of my eye, I see half a Styrofoam cup floating up to shore.

"Where did that come from?" I ask.

She turns to look. "Oh, they wash up all the time."

"But we are thousands of miles away from civilization and the monotonous grind of daily living in the post-Industrial Age." I tell her, "How can there be Styrofoam way out here?"

"Styrofoam is everywhere. It never disintegrates. And it floats." She sighs.

"But this is a fantasy!" I shout, "My fantasy. I don't want Styrofoam cups here!"

"Sorry," she says, lowering herself back into the sea and swimming away.

After that I got up from the lounge. The sun had gone behind the clouds anyway. It looked like it might snow.

Needless to say, I have the environment on my mind. I wash and re-use plastic bags. Line dry my clothes. Buy organic. But the more I do, the trickier it becomes.

Ecologically conscious shopping is riddled with obstacles. Do I choose the fresh, locally grown salsa in a non-biodegradable plastic tub or the commercial salsa in a recyclable jar? Do I purchase Slip-and-Slide Lubricant and support gay-owned enterprise or Gooey-Glide lubricant which isn't tested on animals? Or do I just mindlessly buy Sappo Hill Soap because it's inexpensive, nicely shaped and Sappo sounds like Sappho?

Here's a problem I struggle with: Once a month, my local food store, Crystal Market, holds 5% day, a day during which five percent of all sales go to groups like Safehouse, Greenpeace or the Prairie Grass Defense Fund. I try to stock up on groceries on these days to support the various causes. Sometimes my lover and I go without laundry detergent, safflower oil, cumin or tempeh for a week or more, eagerly awaiting 5% day.

When I am already downtown on that day, it's easy to pop in and load up on stuff. But on some 5% days, I'm tied up at my office (which is in my house) and I have to make a special trip to shop. At first glance, that extra trip seems like a reasonable idea, especially since by now we are out of nine essential household items. But then I consider the environmental impact on prairie grass caused by making an extra trip in my atmosphere-polluting car. Is it worth it?

Take public transportation, you say? Ever try hauling groceries six blocks in a backpack, duffel bag and shoulder bag to the bus station, only to miss the bus? So I wait for the next bus. And watch my frozen organic peas thaw, my Ben & Jerry's ice cream melt. By the time I change buses and drag it all home, I find two of my organic eggs from free-roaming chickens have cracked, my pesticide-free peanut butter has slid out of its non-recyclable plastic tub and my soy milk carton's been squashed by my phosphate-free laundry detergent.

And who do you blame for such a catastrophe? Big corporate greedheads. While it can't make your broken organic eggs whole, it's important to know that in the 1930's, GM, Standard Oil, Phillips Petroleum, Firestone and Mack Truck set up an illegal trust to systematically destroy public transportation systems.

These guys were breaking laws and ruining public transportation for us grocery shoppers, but the federal courts, after finding them guilty in 1949, only gave them measly $1000 fines! This permitted them to continue the practice into the 1960's.

So, here we are, in the '90's, without reliable public transportation, missing buses, watching our socially conscious ice cream melt. It's an outrage.

Okay, okay! you say. Take the car, it's only a short trip. After much agonizing I tried this once. I finally drove to Crystal Market, only to find that I had the wrong day. Five percent day was the *next* Wednesday.

Now what? Do I go another week without cooking oil and laundry detergent? Or do I say to hell with it and buy now? Or do I grab twelve rolls of recycled toilet paper (10% post-consumer content) and toss them madly over the shelves of nonirradiated canned goods?

I could use a break from all this. Maybe a week or so with my lesbian mermaid on our tropical island. And I promise not to bring any Styrofoam cups.

CASHING IN ON PRIDE DAY

It happened to the Sixties. It happened to the Bicentennial and to Earth Day. And now it's our turn. Yes, friends, it's time to commercialize the Lesbian and Gay Pride Day.

Let's face it: this is America and in America passing up an opportunity for commercial exploitation is unheard of. This being the case, I am happy to announce Pride Day Products—items for the most discriminating of lesbians and gay men.

So, in the quest for continued visibility, we offer the following bumper stickers. First, the all-purpose model:

For those in a relationship:

Radical lesbian feminists and ACT-UP activists may enjoy this one:

> ## I'd rather be protesting

We think it looks best on slightly beat-up Honda Civic hatchbacks (1982 models or earlier).

For monogamous 12-Steppers, this one:

> ## One Gay at a Time

Of course, what would a merchandise line be without tacky T-shirts? This is my personal favorite:

For those who wish to express their Pride less publicly, we have snow-scene paperweights. Just turn them upside down, shake, set them down and enjoy. Model NYC69 portrays the Stonewall Uprising, complete with miniature gay men and lesbians pelting the New York vice squad with coins.

A parade of happy homosexuals and their proud P-FLAG

parents is depicted in model SF89, a recreation of the 1989 San Francisco Pride March. A great gift for supportive parents. (And what a thoughtful way to break the news if you aren't yet out to them.)

Romantics might want to give model KW to a loved one. It portrays a same-gender couple kissing beneath a palm tree in Key West. (Indicate male/female preference when ordering.)

As far as gay commercial exploitation goes, I'm not the only one thinking along these lines. You've probably heard that Mattel recently released a Barbie Doll who is an Animal Rights Activist. (She comes with an endangered-species panda bear.)

Well, I'm delighted to break the news that in honor of the twenty-first anniversary of the Stonewall Uprising, Mattel will be introducing Lesbian Barbie™ in three new markets. In its press release, Mattel cited the rise in the number of lesbian mothers and its desire to be on the cutting edge of civil rights.

This first Lesbian Barbie is an executive for a non-profit corporation. Her look is similar to the past, except that her shoes are low pumps instead of high heels. Also, two fingernails on her right hand are short.

Executive Barbie's briefcase includes a jammed date book, an address book filled with a disproportionate amount of women's phone numbers, and two tickets for an Olivia Cruise. Also included is a miniature framed photograph of Midge, her committed partner, for Barbie's miniature executive desk.

Lesbian Barbie's dream house is a remodeled Victorian with suggestive Georgia O'Keeffe posters. Her two lesbian cats— Sheba and Amelia—are posed in adorable positions and never need a litter box. Lesbian Barbie has converted the basement of her home into an apartment which she rents to Skipper, who's just out of the closet. Skipper says Barbie has sold out to the corporate establishment. Barbie dismisses Skipper as a naive baby dyke. Skipper counters that Barbie is ageist. It's an on-going feud.

If you're looking to invest further in the Lesbian Barbie™

line, you might consider purchasing the "Barbie Support Group" package: it comes with four dolls and a therapist. (The safe, supportive office space is sold separately.)

If you are wondering what happened to Ken, don't worry. After years of fantasizing, Ken got together with G.I. Joe. They were last seen driving off together in a Jeep. There was even a "Honk If You're Queer" bumper sticker on the back fender.

THE GIRLS OF SUMMER

Dyke softball. Those girls of summer have beckoned to me and once again I am out at the ball field. The anticipation, the timing, the split-second decisions, the quick moves.

And what position do I play, you ask? Hey, I'm not talking about the moves on the field. I'm talking about the action in the stands, where I'm surrounded front, back and sides by cheering, chatting, flirting women. *That's* what brings me out to the ball game.

Tonight is a good night: with two lesbian teams playing each other the stands are packed and camaraderie is high. The Hag Pack, easy-going ball players known to occasionally wear skirts on the field, is playing Crazy About Softball, a team sponsored by a well-to-do lesbian psychotherapist.

Tonight's also a big night because I've brought my girlfriend, who I'm trying to win over to the art of fandom. She's puzzled by the on-going chatter and extended debates in the stands.

"Does *your* underwear match your socks?" howls a woman three rows up. It's not clear who the question is intended for, but another woman yells out "Can you prove it?" while Katriana, a local activist, asks, "And is it a fashion statement or political statement if it does?" A half dozen responses follow.

My lover comments, "No one is even watching the game. You all could just meet in someone's living room."

Just then Diane catches a line drive and everyone goes wild, screaming and shouting. "Ah," Vicki points out to my lover, "you can't scream like *that* in someone's living room. Besides, out here no one has to play hostess."

Yes, softball may be the perfect form of entertainment. You can show up early or late or miss a week or two and still enjoy yourself. Depending on your mood, you can socialize, gossip, or just hang out and watch the game. It's free and, unlike a party, you can bring along as many friends as you like. And since you never know who'll show up, it's exciting to see who's at the game each week. Plus, you get to watch sunsets over the foothills, just as the day cools down. For me, softball is like the mythical corner store. Drop in, stay awhile, head home.

Oh, sure, it has its problems. Like this, for instance: you're at a game on your second date with Ginny, and who appears from Santa Fe but Carri, your old girlfriend.

"Just popped up for the weekend," she says, giving you a forced smile, but scowling openly at Margie two rows down. Margie—she's the woman you went to bed with just before you and Carri broke up for good—nods curtly. She's mad at you for dating Ginny, on whom she's had a crush for years.

Of course, Ginny is wondering just who *is* this Carri woman with the howling coyote bolo tie anyway? But then *she* spots her ex-roommate Emily, who everyone thought had dropped off the face of the earth. Now, Emily's dropping off the face of the earth was fine with her because Emily was an overzealous, neo-Baptist lesbian politico who relentlessly argued that coming out meant nothing if you weren't born again.

But most of the time it's just fine. Really. What with all those wonderful women in shorts and tank tops, it's an outstanding opportunity to check out tattoos or run your fingers through a new buzz cut. And, to be perfectly honest, we don't *really* ignore those women on the field. We yell out, "Hey Denice, nice shorts!" or comment to the woman next in line to bat, "Great socks, Ardelle. Didn't know it was humanly possible to create such a color." We're sure this helps them concentrate on the game.

Often, as we engage in a myriad of conversations (*A closeted Gay Pride T-shirt, are you kidding? Get this, they're going to couples counseling with a straight male therapist!*), our team makes a double play and we miss it.

"Oh, no," Patrice groans, "was that JoJo? God, if it was JoJo who made that catch, and I missed it, I'll never hear the end of it. Did anyone see the play?"

To alleviate such problems, we created the role of "designated watcher," a woman who, on a rotating basis, watches the game closely. So, if Amanda is busy making camping plans with Dottie and misses her lover's stupendous play in left field, she merely turns to the designated watcher who fills her in. Now, after the game, Amanda can run up to her lover and exclaim, "Honey, what a great catch during the third inning. You made such a decisive dive towards the ball!" The practice of designated watcher has saved countless relationships.

When I'm in a less social, more contemplative mood, I actually like to watch the game. Some women have said that softball is too competitive and patriarchal. I tell them to watch the ball as it arches through the air. From pitcher to batter to fielder to basewoman, its curves are a joyful reminder of a woman's body.

"Oh yeah?" the doubters counter, "What about the bat? Looks pretty phallic to me."

To them I say, "Sure, the woman needs the bat to start out, but once she hits the ball, what's the first thing she does? Drops that bat, right then and there. You don't use the bat to run from base to base, and you *certainly* don't need it to score!"

Besides, everyone knows a diamond is a girl's best friend.

NURTURING INNER SUSPICION

There's a new threat to those of us living in progressive cities, and it isn't drug wars, crumbling infrastructures or hazardous waste. The threat I'm talking about is Adult Education.

Let's face it: Adult Education is everywhere and it's getting worse. Times used to be that Adult Ed meant an innocent water-color class or "Refinishing Furniture for Beginners"—courses taught through the local high school.

Not so anymore. These days anyone can be a teacher. And anyone with a computer can throw together a course catalog. It's a deadly combination.

The worst offenders in the Adult Education field are those self-improvement, personal-growth type catalogs. Now, don't get me wrong—I'm not an advocate of the American Medical Association or the psychiatrist's couch. I've been massaged and Rolfed. I've been empowered through self-defense classes and feminist psychotherapy. I even have my energy field cleared periodically. However, as I flip through these "instant therapy" catalogs, my bewilderment grows and my trust level slips.

One popular workshop is the kind that promises everything—in three hours. The description often reads like this:

SELF-LOVE:
Enhance Your Personal, Sexual, Social, Spiritual and Financial Life and Lose Weight While Doing It.

This workshop builds self-esteem through the power of orgasmic energy and the psychic decision-making process. While reducing anxiety over food and food-related issues, we will explore the spiritual rewards of positive cash flow and resolve the conflicts of living in the nuclear age. Self-empowerment, self-image, self-awareness, self-growth—do it all while strengthening your personal boundaries. Wear comfortable clothing.

Then there are the classes which have fallen victim to the "buzzword" sensation. They focus in on whatever's popular at the moment:

Heal and reconnect with the cosmic anger of your co-dependent inner child through visualization, dream work and meditation. Make life-positive, pro-active choices by repatterning unhealthy, addictive and dysfunctional operative modes. Through the intimate process of re-birthing in pairs, rebuild a loving relationship with your ex-husband, no matter what kind of jerk he's been. Discover your inner goddess, unleash your sacred fire, contemplate planetary transmutation. Bring a bag lunch.

And finally, there are workshops that are so unbelievable that they just can't be classified, on this or any other plane of existence. When courses (such as the one whose description I've plagiarized below) are taught through the local Parks Department, it's easy to understand why America is in a state of cultural decline.

THE SCARF ENCOUNTER
Do you wistfully pass the scarf counter, wishing you

knew how to accessorize with lovely silk squares and charming chalis scarves? Do you too believe that you could dramatically enhance your life if you *only* knew how to turn that basic suit or dress into a fantastic, versatile addition to your wardrobe? Join us and learn to emphasize the classic, the dramatic and the romantic aspects of your true self. Bring three scarves from your own wardrobe to class.

I often wonder what the next stage will be. Choosing a preschool for your inner child? Accessorizing your chakras? Perhaps herbal remedies for your personal computer. Or maybe, Creative Apathy for a More Peaceful Existence. Creative Apathy... wait a minute, folks, I think we have a new threat on our hands.

STUMBLING OVER YOUR NEXT STEP
(BUT TAKING IT ANYWAY)

Once again, it's Coming Out Day, the day when you gather your strength and nerve and take your next step on the rocky road of lesbian and gay visibility.

Let's drop in on Clara as she prepares to tell her co-worker Ruth that she is a lesbian. They are at lunch and dessert has just arrived.

Clara musters up her courage and says, "What I have to tell you is difficult for me to talk about."

"Yes?," says Ruth, concerned.

"I am, that is, I'm. . ." Clara hesitates, "a lesbian."

"Uh, huh," Ruth says, coaxing her on.

"That's it."

"That's it? But I've known *that* for years."

"What? You know? Why didn't you tell me you knew?"

"Well you seemed so private about it."

"I don't believe it! I've been meticulous about not letting anything slip. I've been super vague about my personal life. Every day on my guard and now you tell me—"

Let this scenario be a lesson to all of you who've been agonizing for years. Most of your friends figured it out long ago!

Of course, there are times when we're overtly visible, hoping they'll get the message. Let's say, for example, your mom is coming to town. You figure, "Once she sees my apartment, she'll know I'm a dyke and we can finally talk about it."

So Mom arrives at your place and wanders around. She examines the snapshots on your fridge—pictures of your hike up Mt. Audubon with 17 other lesbians, the New Year's Eve Dance (you in a dress, your ex in a tux). She peruses your bookcase: *The Coming Out Stories, On Being Gay, Lesbian Therapy and You.* She eyeballs your Sinister Wisdom poster and your *Dykes to Watch Out For* calendar.

Finally she says, "Honey, come sit. We need to talk."

"Yeah, Mom?" you say, ready to spill your heart.

"Your cousin Benny's got a friend out here, Walter. A very nice fellow. Maybe you could call him up, go out on a date. . ."

"Arghhhhh!!" (A guttural scream, in case you couldn't tell.)

But can we blame them for being oblivious? After all, how many of us spent months or years denying our own sexuality when it was right there, staring us in the face?

I'll be the first to confess. When I was 13, my older sister got a copy of *Our Bodies, Ourselves.* First chance I got, I stole it out of her bedroom. I read about female sexuality, reproduction, then I got to the chapter, "In Amerika They Call Us Dykes." I read it, then read it again.

"I'm interested in it from a sociological point of view," I told myself. During the next five years I probably reread that section a dozen times, never thinking that I related to it because I was also gay. (I didn't dare use the "L" word yet.)

I know I'm not the only one. C'mon, raise your hands. How many of you read that chapter twenty times over? My favorite story was about two women who stayed up late talking, then laid down on a bed together, head to toe. One gets up to check on her car; when she lies down again, this time it's *head to head.* A gentle yet passionate scene ensues.

That story never left me, and *still* it wasn't until I was 25 that I finally figured out that I was a lesbian.

And then there's my lover Lori, who at age 21 thought she *might* be a lesbian. She did what was natural for her— went out and bought ten books on the subject. After reading them all, she decided she could go either way and that being straight was easier.

Three years later—surprise, surprise—the question of sexual orientation again arose. This time, friends at work were happy to facilitate the process. First, Joan invited Lori to a party. Lori watched women coming in pairs and thought, "Isn't it great that they are such good friends?"

Then another friend, Randy, lent Lori a Meg Christian tape, with *Leaping Lesbians* recorded three times on it. Lori figured that Randy liked Meg Christian's music, but she just knew that Randy couldn't be a lesbian herself.

Finally, Randy bought her a Meg Christian concert ticket. Before the show started, Randy leaned over and gave her lover Donna a long kiss.

"Wait a minute," Lori thought, "I get it. These women are lovers. These women are lesbians."

Yes, it's a great day when we start recognizing that we are everywhere. At my first CU Lady Buffs basketball game, I didn't believe my friend Kathy when she kept pointing out groups of women and saying, "Now there's a bunch of dykes. And those two horsing around over there certainly are." No, I didn't believe her then. Now I do.

One last thing. If you're fresh out of ideas for what to do this Coming Out Day, I invite you to send this essay to a friend or relative to whom you are not yet out. Attach a Post-It note declaring: "Guess what? I'm one too." (Don't forget to sign your name!)

Whatever your next step, whatever your degree of visibility, Happy Coming Out Day! It's good to have you in the family.

CORPORATE ODYSSEY

I had an unsettling experience this autumn. No, my cat did not run away from home, I wasn't suddenly attracted to men, nor did I have an unexpected urge to vote Republican. No, this was *really* odd. What happened to me was that I was hired to work in Corporate America.

"Ellen!" I hear all you faithful readers exclaiming, "You're a hard-core, independent self-employed graphic artist, activist and writer. Corporate America? How could this have possibly occurred?"

Well, I have to admit that I *did* interview for the position. It's not like they called me up out of the blue and said, "Hey, hear you've got a good eye for design, why don't you work for us?"

I saw the classified ad, called them up, sent a resume, the whole spiel. Eventually, I interviewed with a woman in "Human Resources," which is the corporate term for "office that hires people." Human Resources? Let me guess, pieces of coal and sulphur interview with "Mineral Resources" when they're looking for a job.

Anyway, the first thing I did when I found out I'd been granted an interview was to update and rearrange my portfolio, a relatively easy task. The tricky part came next: I had to a buy a dress.

Fortunately I'm one of those lesbians who can wear a dress without looking like an amateur drag queen. This fact made the process easier. I trooped over to the local mall, tried on a bunch of dresses and settled for one that was professional enough to wear to a job interview, yet stylish enough to wear to a hetero-sexual social event. (Since those are the only two times in life when I put on a dress, and neither comes up all that frequently, I figured it had better be a multi-purpose garment.)

When I got the dress home, I unearthed my black pumps, a pair of nylons, and a few pieces of conservative jewelry. Putting everything on, I walked into the living room and asked Lori, "What do you think?"

She looked up from her book and asked, "Who are you?"

"C'mon," I said, "I need your opinion here."

"Okay." she replied, "You look like an entirely different woman."

"How so?" I countered.

"You look cool and reserved, like a high-powered profes-sional who'd never in a million years use the word 'dyke' to describe herself."

"Well, I guess that will work," I said, and wandered back to the bedroom to pull on a pair of sweat pants and my lesbian vampire T-shirt.

Later as I was washing the dishes, I turned to Lori and said, "Honey, I have something I want to tell you. I've made a decision on a difficult matter. I don't want to debate it, but I do want your support on it."

Lori turned noticeably pale. "You've fallen in love with another woman and you're leaving me."

"Of course not, I—"

"You've decided to have a baby."

"What?! No, it's—"

"You want to move back to New Jersey."

"Would you hold on a second? I've decided to shave my legs

for the interview, and I don't want any grief about it, that's all!"

"Oh." Then a pause. "That's it?! All that dramatic build up for a pair of shaved legs? Really, Ellen."

(Disclaimer: Much of the above dialogue was fictionalized slightly—okay, a lot—to improve its dramatic effect. P.S. Lori made me write this disclaimer.)

Meanwhile, back to the story.

After buying a six-pack of plastic razors (the cheapest way to buy them, oddly enough), the next day I set about soaping up and shaving my legs. "What a waste of time," I thought, "glad I don't do this on a regular basis."

As I rinsed off the blade for the twelfth time, I quickly calculated in my head. "Hmm, at five gallons per shave and three shaves per week, wow, we hairy-legged gals save over 700 gallons of water each year by not shaving. The socio-ecological implications are astounding."

While I shaved, I also thought of Marga Gomez, a comedienne I'd heard at the Albuquerque Women's Music Festival. She had a great story about her "interview pantyhose" which she faithfully dragged out for each interview she went through. Once she landed the job, however, the hose were gone and the pants back on.

At the same festival, another woman mentioned a trick *she'd* learned. Instead of shaving her legs for interviews, she doubled up on the pantyhose. "Hides the hair completely," she attested.

So, with my new dress and bald legs I went in, interviewed, and got the job. And, like Marga, my nylons have not appeared since.

So, what do I do? What is life like in Corporate America for an off-the-wall activist like myself? Is it true that I've got pictures of five gay men and seven lesbians on my office walls? A postcard of Amelia Earhart on my computer?

To find out for sure, tune in to this same column for the future adventures of "Radical Dyke in Corporate America."

THE "S" WORD

This essay is about sex. Lesbian sex.

But before you get too fired up, let me warn you that I'm not out to sexually excite, thrill or titillate you. (Titillate—now there's an interesting word. Derived from the action of elating one's tits, I suppose.)

No, this column isn't going to contain any passionate passages or sensual sentences such as. . .

> As the waterfall spilled forth beside them, splashing drops on their already flushed skin, Yvette looked deeply into Illana's eyes. Her nipples swelled as she reached out to wipe the spray from Illana's cheek, feeling an intense desire surging deep inside her.

Nope, no provocative paragraphs here. Just serious questions.

First Question

Despite all our talk about theoretical sex, how come nobody discusses the particulars of their own sex lives? Do *your* friends ask you, "I was wondering, do you think making love twice a month is enough?" or casually remark, "You know, I get really excited when my lover chews on my thighs. What do you get off on?"

Why we don't talk about our sex lives? Does it have to do with confidentiality? Loyalty? Are they the same thing?

I've always had the impression that straight women get together and compare notes on their husbands and boyfriends. This is easy for them because their female friends aren't close with their male lovers.

But with lesbians, our friends are often friends with our lovers. (In fact, our friends are often ex-lovers of our lovers.) Sharing the intimacies of our sex lives, therefore, is a tricky juggling act involving honesty, confidentiality and—of course— boundaries.

And then there's the loyalty question. Lesbians don't have the "us" and "them" situation that heterosexual folks do. It is all "us." If a lesbian has problems with her lover, it can't be neatly blamed as a "male" shortcoming. It is *our* issue.

Sometimes, it feels heretical to the institution of lesbianism to say, "I really don't like oral sex," or "Sex was somehow more exciting with Wally." But if this is so, are we then defining sex as the foundation of lesbian culture? And if *this* is so, is this whole essay starting to sound like a bad parody of a circa 1971, late-night consciousness-raising group?

Ah, what to do? First of all, drop the "loyalty to lesbian sex" bit. Sex between women has been around for millions of years, and can certainly withstand a little bandying about.

And concerning the confidentiality part—well, in a couples' situation, it's a good idea to keep some people as primarily Partner A's friends and confidants, and other people as Partner B's friends and confidants. It's helpful to establish who Partner B feels comfortable having Partner A talk to.

If you're part of a non-monogamous couple or a monoga- mous threesome, use the same recipe as above, but add partners (or sub-partners) C, D, and E as needed. Shake well and keep notes.

Second Question

While I rarely talk specifically about sex, somehow I know an awful lot about the sex lives of people whose sex lives I'd just as soon not know about. Honestly, people tell me the most personal stuff about other people. Do I really need to know that Jody is very loud when she comes, or Stephanie has orgasms quickly and easily, or Zola had a two-week affair with Sarina while her lover was out of town? This information gets passed around until everyone except the gossipees (those folks whom the gossip is about) are in on the dirt.

Eventually, I find myself talking to the gossipee, who is still being vague about the subject. What should I do? Should I say, "Look, Louise, everyone knows you have a complex swash-buckler fantasy that you indulge in the second time you make love with someone on a new moon. You don't have to refer to it as 'this special activity,' okay?"

You might have the guts to say that, but me? I just nod my head and smile.

A Question About S/M

Once upon a time, lesbian S/M sex was considered politically incorrect and offensive. But then it became very vogue in these parts to read about and discuss S/M. It was stylish to be enlightened and open-minded about it, and to remember to say SM and not S and M. Then, a year or so back, it again became trendy to criticize S/M as unhealthy and repressive.

I can't say I have any fresh or insightful opinions about S/M, but I do have my difficulties with one part of it—the "scenes" or fantasies.

Now, for the record, I am aware that scenes in and of themselves are not necessarily S/M-related nor does S/M always involve scenes. (I am relatively hip to the theory, if not the practice, of S/M).

Anyway, as I was saying, I find the idea of complex fantasies problematic. I can imagine going home with a really hot woman who is into scenes, and by the time we (I? she?—I don't know who'd be the script writer here) decide that the setting is an ancient Greek island on a beach after a long day of gazelle hunting and she's an honored huntress and I'm a decathlon champion... quite frankly, it would be two in the morning and we'd only have time for a quick good night kiss before falling into an exhausted sleep.

Or even if we started at eleven in the morning and time wasn't an issue, I can imagine becoming terribly confused. As she approached me draped only in green silk and an orange wig, I would undoubtedly kill the moment by blurting out, "Wait! Are we on the Planet Zarconia and you're the captain of the spaceship, or is this the sunken continent of Atlantis and you're a sea serpent?"

I can imagine it now. She'd toss me out of the house and immediately call up her ex-lover and babble on about my ineptitude. By noon the next day everyone in the metro Denver area would know about it.

And I'd still be wondering—spaceship captain or sea serpent?

WAR, WORK AND WORRY

As I write this, our country is at war. Our air force is bombing Baghdad, Iraq's military is shooting missiles at Israel. Millions of civilians are fleeing, and a huge oil slick is smothering seabirds and coral reefs.

It's a difficult time to write funny stuff.

Friends assure me that our government has been supporting war and terrorism for decades now, that U.S.-sponsored destruction and killing go on daily, that this is no different, only more obvious. If this is meant to comfort me, it doesn't.

Before the war started, a friend of mine proposed that Bush and Hussein go off to a small room together. I figured she'd say that the two of them should just slug it out. But no. Instead she suggested that they go into the room, close the door, pull down their pants, and compare penis sizes. Whoever's was bigger would be declared the winner and everybody could go home.

A friend's therapist had another creative alternative. Put Bush and Hussein on a 72-hour hold for psychiatric observation. Trained experts would determine if they were a danger to themselves or others. If they were found to be a threat (and undoubtedly they would be) they could be locked up for a few decades.

Of course, our military did go to war. (What? You expect them to be original and do something different?) Immediately, a wave of nationalism hit, symbolized, oddly enough, by polyester American flags (made in Taiwan) and plastic yellow ribbons. Since polyester and plastic are petroleum-based products, manufacturing them uses up the oil that thousands are dying for. Talk about mixed messages.

Countering this boosterism are continuing peace demonstrations, with large lesbian and gay contingents. Signs like "Dykes and Fags Against Body Bags" and "Fight AIDS, not Iraq" are cropping up all over.

Unfortunately these rallies have been dominated by straight, upper-middle-class white men who scream at us to get involved. Get involved? Where have *they* been for the last fifteen years? Certainly not at the pro-choice rallies, not at the lesbian and gay freedom marches, and not at ACT-UP protests.

While I stood there listening to the speeches—the wind whipping my "Another Lesbian for Peace" poster to shreds—it occurred to me why Bush waited until January to launch the attack. It didn't have anything to do with military strategy. He just wanted the protesters to freeze.

Many people have noted that a big casualty of this war is language. Jets no longer run bombing missions; instead "sorties" are flown. What the hell is a "sortie" anyway? It sounds like a new line of frozen desserts. And surgical strikes? Let me guess —heart surgeons walking the picket line. Hey, let's call it like it is: killing, maiming, destroying.

So, the war goes on, brought to you by Our Tax Dollars. This is particularly ironic for me, since I recently began a job at which I make just enough money to lose a huge percentage of it to taxes.

It's true. I work in a large concrete and glass structure with sealed windows. I sit in front of a low-frequency radiation-emitting computer screen, the effects of which upon the human molecular structure are, as of yet, undetermined.

I also go to meetings. We discuss what to write and how to

write it. Then I go back to my desk and I write. My work gets edited. I rewrite. Then it gets passed around for criticism, after which I rewrite again. Eventually it gets shown to the guys at the top, who have entirely different ideas, and the process starts over.

You'd think this would drive everyone crazy, and it would, except that the board of directors, one step ahead of us, has shrewdly equipped the lunch room with sugar and caffeine dispensers. Others call them candy and soda pop machines, but regardless of the name, they are heavily relied upon to chemically control one's frustration, boredom and fatigue. Of course there are a few hold-outs who instead turn to herbal tea and carob Power Bars.

Sometimes, as I sit at work, rearranging words and flexing my mouse hand, I muse that this war will become nuclear in a few weeks, the world will be blown up and I'll have spent my last days moving tiny words around a screen in a concrete and glass building with sealed windows.

Can you tell that I have doubts about this job? I've considered sharing these hesitations with my supervisor, telling her, "Working here has tempted me to move to Upper Mantoobia, take up sheep herding and live off the land in solidarity with the native vegetation." But I don't say this, knowing she'd just look me in the eye and tell me I have an "attitude problem."

I could share my troubles with my lover, now a psychotherapy graduate student at The Naropa Institute, a Buddhist-inspired school. I could tell her "honey, I spend all day moving lines of text up and down a screen in order to create a reference manual for yet one more word-processing program in a world which already has thousands of perfectly adequate word-processing programs, when we all should junk these computers and relearn the ancient art of cuneiform."

I could tell her this, except that she's heard similar whining from me a hundred times. Anyway, I'm afraid she'd just tell me that I'm expressing "negative negativity," which is a Buddhist way of saying I have an "attitude problem."

But, you know, maybe more of us should develop an attitude problem. Develop it and take it to the streets. And to the politicians, to the newspapers, to each other. Maybe then we can move forward towards peace and justice... for all.

SOME LIKE IT HOT

As I settle into these cold winter nights, my thoughts turn to hot—no, not hot sex (at least not all the time)—but to hot tea. A steaming mug of tea and a good book, or good conversation, or at least a good rerun of Star Trek.

For those of us who live in Boulder, it is politically correct, if not practically mandatory, to stock Celestial Seasonings tea in your kitchen. And I do mean stock. One box of Red Zinger just doesn't cut it. You need to have a full selection of fruity, minty and spicy teas. You *can* get a sampler pack, but real dykes have whole boxes of each. Whole boxes, which in many cases, have been around longer than a lot of preschoolers I know.

Choosing which tea to drink is practically a ritual, what with trying to match the tea flavor to your current mood or to the image you want to project. Hoping for a quiet evening with your lover? Choose Almond Sunset. Attempting to be seductive for your date? Try Bengal Spice; it's got a tiger on the package. Want to appear vivacious and free-spirited at your first party since you and your girlfriend split up? Go for "Tropical Escape."

If you resist making a choice, instead offering an offhand comment like, "anything minty will be fine," your hostess will undoubtedly retort, "Peppermint, Mellow Mint, Spearmint, Tummy Mint, or Mint Magic?" Not surprisingly, there are certified cases of emotional breakdowns resulting from the pressure of deciding which of the 120 different flavors to choose. And this from teas that are supposed to be soothing.

But barring anything this extreme, you eventually choose a flavor and pop the tea bag of choice into a mug of hot water, which sits next to four other steeping mugs. Inevitably, when the mugs are passed around, no one remembers which tea bag went into which mug and instead of getting Lemon Zinger you get Roastaroma. However, everyone is either too busy flirting or too politically enwrapped to notice.

Of course, not everyone can relate to this "celestial" lifestyle. One time, I had a bunch of lesbians over to my house to help with a newsletter mailing. One woman brought a large plastic bottle of diet Coke for all of us to share. I put it on the counter where it was forgotten. About a half hour later, the woman got up to pour herself some of the now-warm soda pop, and asked for ice cubes.

"We don't have any," I said, trying unsuccessfully to explain that we had one of those self-defrosting freezers that cause ice cubes to evaporate due to some law of thermodynamics and advanced refrigeration that I don't fully comprehend. The idea of having no ice cubes appeared to be extremely foreign to her, even suspect, so I changed tactics and offered her something hot to drink.

"Fine," she said, "I'll have coffee."

"Uh, we don't have any." I said, not wanting to explain that we really didn't do caffeine at our house.

"No coffee?" she said, aghast. "I don't need anything fancy. Instant is fine."

"Sorry. How about some tea?" I suggested, figuring that at least in this department I was prepared.

"That would be fine."

"Great. What flavor?" I asked.

"Flavor?" she repeated. "Just tea, regular tea."

"Sorry," I mumbled, "we don't have any." I finally ended up making her a cup of peppermint tea. She never did return to any of our subsequent mailing parties.

Anyway, back to Celestial Seasonings. A couple of years ago, they branched into the production of gourmet caffeinated teas, in order to gain a larger market share. This is all well and good, but as I perused their shelf of teas at the store recently, I realized that Celestial Seasonings is still missing a lot of people out there.

Consider, if you will, the names of these teas. Cranberry *Cove*, Strawberry *Fields*, Blackberry *Forest*, Raspberry *Patch*. Don't their market researchers realize there are a lot of city people who just don't relate to coves, fields, forests and patches?

Therefore, I humbly suggest to Celestial's Board of Directors, a new product line: Celestial Seasoning's Urban Teas—with names like Hibiscus Highrise, Raspberry Rent Control or Ginseng Jackhammer.

Think I'm crazy, don't you? Just you wait. In a couple of years, a good friend of yours will fly in from Los Angeles. Just before the two of you settle into evening of catching up, you'll offer her some hot tea.

"Sounds good," she'll say, "How about some Peppermint Parking Lot or Tangerine Tollbooth?"

"Sorry," you'll have to say, feeling like a failed hostess, "we don't have any."

DON'T TOUCH THAT REMOTE!

I confess. I like TV commercials. A creative, overactive brain like mine has a field day with them—especially when the sound is off. You've just gotta know how to improve 'em.

One of my favorites is a gourmet coffee commercial. Two women are sitting together on a boat, sipping their coffee, enjoying the sunrise, professing their devout friendship for each other.

Just when you think it's going to get interesting, one of them says, "Should we wake the guys?"—a line which assures us, in case anyone was getting nervous, that these women are straight.

In her best conspiratorial tone, the other says, "No, let's keep this all to ourselves."

"Ha, ha, those girls are feisty," the viewers chuckle, "though not dangerous to the moral fiber of this great nation."

Now let's hit the mute button and open up a *lot* more possibilities. Okay, the women (we'll call them Krista and Jenny) are still on the boat, still watching the sunrise, but. . .

Krista: A perfect morning! A brilliant sunrise, a cup of General Thrills Swiss Mocha®, and a good friend. What more could one ask for?

Jenny: Now that you mention it, I have an incredible crush on you and want to make passionate love right here, right now on the deck of this boat.

Krista: Think we should wake the guys?

Jenny: No. I want this moment all to ourselves. Besides, I threw them both overboard last night.

Krista: Oh, so *that's* what that splashing was all about. Well, darling, I'm all yours. Come give me a long, deep kiss.

VOICEOVER: *General Thrills International Coffees. Celebrate the moments of your life.*

Now, sometimes, turning off the sound and making up new words doesn't help a bit. One such case in point is a truly offensive commercial for Mazda's latest truck, the Navajo. Not surprisingly, members of the Navajo community are ticked off about the name of this vehicle. To name *any* automobile after the Navajo people—much less an off-road vehicle that tears up the fragile ecoscape—is a disgrace.

But wait. It gets worse. You see, the commercial is one of those high-tech types, filled with fleeting images that aren't even necessarily part of the Navajo culture. It goes like this: Picture of the southwest desert. Click! Off-road vehicle zips up the road. Switch shots. A kiva, with a ladder emerging. Back to the truck: a close-in shot of a brawny Caucasian male at the wheel. Flash! A petroglyph etched on a canyon wall. Cut back to brawny man, who whips vehicle past sunset, then brakes with testosterone-filled precision. He jumps from vehicle, strides toward stereotype of female Native American. Flash! Progressive-minded viewers at home throw up.

There are a lot of reasons to hate this commercial. For starters, it's loaded with "macho man conquers nature and natives" garbage. But I'd like to focus on the kivas, petroglyphs and canyons. These are spiritual images and places. They are what mainstream America calls "religious imagery."

Odd, isn't it, that a car company would use religion to sell its products. Can you imagine them doing that with Christian imagery? Probably not. But I can.

Therefore, I present to you the ultimate high-powered, off-road vehicle. The Presbyterian!

Setting: The Holy Land (where else?). A bright star rises in the east.

Action: Three weary but wise men trudge towards Bethlehem. Appearing out of nowhere, a flashy, aggressive vehicle zooms past them. It's the Presbyterian! With the wise men left choking in the dust, the camera cuts to the tan guy in the driver's seat. He flashes us a perfect white-toothed smile.

Click! The Presbyterian zips past a crowd gathered around a mount. As one, all heads turn away from Jesus to watch instead the truly splendid awe of this miraculous automotive machine.

Flash! The Presbyterian speeds past a group of mourners. Even before Jesus can approach the casket, Lazarus rises from the dead, driven by the desire to catch a brief glimpse of the Presbyterian as it tears on by. The camera cuts to the driver who lowers his shades, throwing us a self-assured, manly look.

Flash! Time for real action: Shifting into four-wheel drive, the driver puts the pedal to the metal and the Presbyterian rips up a rugged hill. Three crosses appear in the distance. It's Calvary!

Boom! The driver brings the vehicle to a screeching halt, leaps out of his seat. As he strides towards the crosses, Mary Magdalene breaks out of the crowd, and runs towards him, arms open wide.

VOICEOVER: *The Presbyterian: With off-road power like this, you don't need a higher power.*

69

WATCHING WOMEN IN ATLANTA

Happy Lesbian and Gay Pride month! (Yes, we've taken over the entire month now.) It's time to celebrate, demonstrate, educate, co-habitate—all in the name of enriching our lives.

And speaking of education and celebration, I'm recently back from the National Lesbian Conference in Atlanta. I'll tell you, there's nothing like landing at the Atlanta airport at 10 pm and arriving at the Radisson at 11 pm only to be told that your room reservation won't be honored because the previous convention of linear-thinking, male-identified scientists was held over.

True, that night the Radisson put us up for free at a hotel across town, but it took about an hour of hard-core negotiating and hassling before everything was settled. The one thing that made it bearable was that the conservative Radisson hotel was filled with very obvious, very out dykes.

Honest to goddess, this is true: the first lesbian my travelling companions and I talked with was named Luna and lived on women's land in the Ozarks. She'd moved to Atlanta six months earlier to help plan the conference. During the conference, there were two times in which I was convinced that I had lost my airline ticket. During these moments of panic, I swore it was a sign that I should renounce my decadent, materialistic lifestyle and join Luna in the Ozarks.

On the first day of the conference I kept thinking I saw women I knew. Then I'd look again and realize I was mistaken. After I experienced this strange phenomenon a few times, I wondered if there were only twelve standard lesbian types in this world, with only the haircuts varying. Fortunately this odd quirk passed, leaving me plenty of time to admire, chat and flirt with the multitude of lesbians pervading the surroundings.

One of my favorite activities was T-shirt watching. First of all, it's a neat way to start a conversation—"Hey, a Model Mugging T-shirt. I took that course. First level. You took the weapons course? Wow, what was it like?"

T-shirt watching is also vastly entertaining. I even started a list of my favorite slogans:

1. Girl Scout Gone Bad
2. Dykes from Hell (with raging flames in the background)
3. U.S. Out of My Uterus
4. A large black and white photo of labia and clitoris, complete with pubic hair. The caption was (of course) "Read My Lips."
5. A picture of a group of nuns with the caption, "Sisters Are Doing It For Themselves."

My single regret of the weekend was that I forgot my "Lesbian Vampires from Sodom" T-shirt. Oh well, next conference.

Almost as much fun as T-shirts were the titles of the workshops and caucuses. The caucuses were informal, leaderless meetings at which women with common interests gathered to talk. For instance, I called a caucus for lesbian writers.

Most of the caucuses focused on issues you'd expect: lesbians with children, interracial couples, lesbian healers, etc. But what caught my attention were the ones that were off the beaten path: lesbians in horticulture; lesbians in uniform (lots of women peeking in the door); lesbian ex-nuns (more women peeking in the door, probably looking for their former Catholic school teachers); and lesbians who were members of the John Birch Society in a past life. (Okay, I made that one up.)

My favorite workshop title was "Breaking Up Isn't Hard— It's Hell!" And then there was "Lobbying and Crystals"; I never did find out what that was all about.

Naturally, where there are lesbians there has to be controversy. Heated battles flared even in the Marketplace, an area where individual women and groups sold all sorts of merchandise. (Actually, this was my favorite part of the conference—the place where I met publishers, writers, and quasi-famous people like Joan Nestle, JEB, Celeste West and my girlfriend's ex-lover.)

Anyway the flap began when someone posted a sign which read, *Lambda Rising Bookstore isn't lesbian-owned. Please support lesbian-owned businesses.*

Of course there were other groups selling merchandise, such as ACT-UP, Queer Nation, and the Human Rights Campaign Fund, which weren't exclusively lesbian either, so it wasn't clear to me why the signs were singling out Lambda Rising. Perhaps it was because there *were* lesbian-owned bookstores there.

A day later, a second flyer appeared on a wall. It read: *Don't assume the woman you are buying from is a lesbian. Ask first.* The next day, another sign appeared below it. It read: *Don't assume the woman you're sleeping with is a lesbian. Ask first.*

And I can't resist mentioning the other posted notice I really enjoyed. It showed up Friday morning, amid the chaos and confusion of 3000 milling lesbians. It read: *L.A. Law update: Abby asked C.J. for a date. C.J. said yes!!!!*

Now, while the queer life might be an uncertainty for Abby, I hope it is crystal clear for you. Happy Pride everyone!

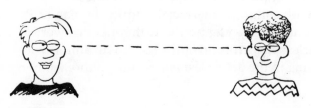

GOING IT ALONE

If I were a smart columnist, I'd have a backlog of funny essays stacked up in my filing cabinet, ready to send to my editor at a moment's notice. That way when extraordinary circumstances arose, I wouldn't miss my deadlines. Instead I'd just zip out an essay and pop it in the mail.

By extraordinary circumstances, I mean situations which make writing difficult. Hypothetically, such instances could be a tornado hitting my Macintosh, me being stricken with the Surillian flu or—still hypothetically speaking, of course—my lover and I breaking up.

Well, all right. That last situation is not particularly hypothetical. In fact, it's quite true. Lori and I really did break up.

However, I don't have a stack of surplus essays and even if I did, I wouldn't use them. After all, many of you have been reading this column since its inception nearly two years ago. You've followed our adventures as Lori and I visited my family in New Jersey, took on homophobes in a hot tub, adjusted our lives as Lori began graduate school and I joined (albeit reluctantly) the corporate world. To quietly drop Lori out of the column without explanation would be deceitful to my sacred vow as an artist and writer. (What? You didn't know that artists and writers took sacred vows? It's true! We're right up there with doctors and nuns.)

Yup, the relationship is over. But you probably already knew that. Everybody else seems to. News travels so fast around here that sometimes I think the lesbian grapevine runs on fiber optics.

(Actually, Lori and I were tempted to test the grapevine theory. We were going to tell one friend of ours that we were splitting up, then see how many hours it took until the whole of Boulder County was in on it.)

Let me mention that several months back, after I first wrote about my new job, a friend asked me if I actually had this new job or if I just made it up to be funny. (I really have the job.) So, in case any of you are wondering if I just made up a lover to add depth to this column, the answer is no. Lori is a real person. (And, for that matter, so am I.)

Lori and I broke up during the week of Pride and the 4th of July. Of course, this is a big time for socializing, and naturally when folks saw me they'd ask how I was and of course I'd have to fill them in. I must have gone through my woeful tale six dozen times in ten days. And while most people were amazingly supportive, I heard an awful lot of this response:

"You've really grown in this relationship. I can tell it's been a true learning experience for you."

If I hear these words one more time, no matter how well-intentioned the person is, I'll throw up on her Reeboks. I've had enough personal growth to last into my mid-40's, thank you very much.

Another comment I've received is, "I know this is a painful time for you, but there are a lot of women out there who'll be glad to learn you're available."

Now, *this* is a terrific response, one I'm always glad to hear. Even if it *is* a boldfaced lie. I don't care. You can tell me this anytime.

In a more philosophical vein, this break up has left me wondering about many things. Does anyone out there know the answers to these questions?

When will I stop instinctively calling Lori "honey" or "sweetheart"? How long does it take to stop saying "we" and start saying "I"? And when will I stop wandering over to the dresser to get the cat brush only to remember that not only is the cat brush gone, but so is the cat? (Actually, there's still one cat left. In fact, our two cats never liked each other. In fact, it's likely that they conspired together to cause this break up.)

And finally, at what point, when I hear noises in the bedroom, will I stop saying to myself, "Oh, that's just Lori rustling around"?

Anyone who knows the answers, please fax them to us—I mean *me*— immediately. I'll be waiting. Thanks.

GOING IT ALONE
PART II

Hah! You thought you'd only have to suffer through *one* essay about breaking up. You thought that *this* month you'd be assured of reading something funny. Like some ironic humor about lesbian sex or Jesse Helms. (Hard to imagine those two in the same thought, isn't it?)

C'mon now. Do you really think it would be fair for you to be happy and giggling while I'm engulfed in the misery and pain of a break up? Yes, it's been rough. And you know what's been the roughest? Not the loneliness or fading self-worth, not the utter shock or bouts of depression. No, the most difficult part of this break up is: I DON'T OWN ANY PLATES.

Why don't I—a 30-year-old woman who's been out on her own for twelve years—own a set of dishes? It's simple: I've always lived with house mates and used their dishes.

Okay, I confess. I do own three plates, but they are boring or silly plates. I got the first one when I moved in with a housemate back in '85. At the time I bought one (1) plate, because I was afraid she wouldn't share her dishes. (She did.) It's navy blue, not a particularly attractive or uplifting plate.

Then there's the cow plate, a gift from my sister. It's a three-dimensional, hand-painted gem with a Holstein prominently molded in high relief upon it. It's so tacky that it's wonderful. And yes, I actually eat off it. However, since I brought this plate to work, it's not available for home use.

Which leaves me with one other plate, a real doozy. A gift from the Oberlin College Alumni Office, it was my prize for being an outstanding alumni class president. It features, even more prominently than the cow, a historical building on the Oberlin Campus, Peters Hall. (Who but a dyke can fully appreciate such a name?)

Now Peters Hall is a neat building and all—lots of turrets and sweeping staircases—and I fondly remember the two sessions I had there at Psych Services. Yes, a male student intern and I tried unsuccessfully to figure out why I felt unromantic around men. He suggested that I initiate a date, i.e., ask a guy out. So I did. I asked out Rich. How was I to know that Rich had a boyfriend, Lee? Of course Lee wasn't concerned in the least about my date with Rich, because they both assumed I was a lesbian. (Aren't inter-gender queer dynamics great?)

Anyhow, just because Peters Hall was a cool old building doesn't mean I want to look at it every time I grab a bite to eat. Plus the plate has a horrid brocade-like trim on it. And besides being ugly, my two plates are always dirty. Every time I fix a bagel or dish out some leftovers, I have to wash a plate.

Now you might be wondering (if you're actually still reading this diatribe on dishes) why on earth I don't buy some new plates with a design I like? Ah, there's the catch: *a design I like.*

What design would I get? Am I in a rational enough state of mind to make such a major decision? I can imagine going to the store in one of my somber, introverted moods and picking out a mottled grey and black service for eight and despising it two days later. Even more likely is that I'd overcompensate and get a super-trendy sunburst teal and magenta confetti pattern that I'd be off-loading at a garage sale next spring.

So, for now, my solution to my plate dilemma is to
a. eat out of cans.
b. eat out of deli containers.
c. hang out at friends' houses until they feed me.

Of course, plates aren't the only thing missing in my life. When she moved out, Lori took all the electronic gadgets: the VCR, the TV, the stereo. Can you imagine such audacity? Oh sure, they were hers, and they'd *been* hers long before she ever met me, but still. . .

The Entertainment
Center

Somehow I keep forgetting I don't have these things any more. Like the other day at work when I was thinking to myself, "Everyone's been telling me to take care of myself. Well, I'm going to do just that. Tomorrow night I'll rent a couple of mindless videos and watch them while I eat my dinner out of deli cartons!"

Then the other inner voice popped up.

"Ellen, you don't *have* a VCR. Got it? We had this discussion last week. You didn't have one then and you don't have one now. So listen carefully. You don't have a VCR. You don't have a VCR. . ."

"All right," I yell back at the voice, "I'll *buy* a VCR. I'll even charge it on my new Gay Credit Union Mastercard!! So there!"

The voice retorted, "Ellen, you don't *have* a TV. You don't *have* a TV."

To hell with it. Who needs high technology anyway? I'll go hang out with friends instead. Maybe they'll even feed me.

AFFIRMATIONS IN ACTION

A few months back, when I was steeped in despair over my break up, I noticed that I wasn't sleeping well, wasn't eating well, wasn't feeling any enthusiasm for life. Fortunately I still retained the presence of mind to recognize the feelings for what they were: symptoms of depression.

The next week I plopped down on my therapist's couch and announced, "I'm clinically depressed."

"Let's not toss around psychological jargon," she replied. "What are you *feeling*?"

"I'm not hungry. Can't sleep. My self-esteem is shot. What's the purpose in living since we all die anyway?"

"Hmm," she said. "Sound's like you're depressed."

I glared in her direction.

"So, what do you want to do about it?" she asked.

"I want to *wallow* in it," I said, acknowledging that the depression had not dulled my sarcasm.

Of course, I didn't *really* want to wallow in it. But how could I get out of it? My brother was always proclaiming the virtues of affirmations, and I figured I could handle listening to an affirmation tape as long as I kept busy doing something else like driving or washing dishes.

So, I took myself to the neighborhood New Age store, Healing and Feeling, and asked the clerk if they carried any tapes of loving affirmations for depressed people wallowing through the aftermath of a break up.

"Over there," she said, pointing to the back of the store. Figuring there'd be maybe a dozen tapes of affirmations, I was bowled over to see a whole wall full of them. Louise Hay had two shelves just to herself: *Healing Your Body; Healing Your Mind; Teaching Your Dog to Heal.*

I eyed other titles as well: *Affirmations for the Joyous Heart, Six Weeks to Inner Peace, Guided Meditations for the Spiritually Inept, Jane Fonda's Seven Chakra Workout.* Nothing seemed right. Besides, at $12.95 each, they were rather pricey.

Then I spotted the discount bin. Rummaging through, I found a pile of tapes by T.J. Hay, Louise's lesser-known lesbian sister.

"Now, I'm getting somewhere," I thought, reading the titles. *Getting Clear, Being Queer; The Inner Journey to Coming Out; Affirmations for the Radiant Clitoris.* I finally chose, *Letting Loose of Your Lesbian Ex-Lover.* At $2.99, I knew I'd gotten a deal.

I trotted home, and popped the cassette into the tape player.

"Hello," a warm and kind voice said, "I'm T.J. Hay and together we're going to let loose of your lesbian ex-lover."

I looked at the tape player. "Right." I said.

"Find yourself a comfortable, safe space. Sit down and relax."

"Forget it," I told T.J., "I'm putting away my laundry."

"That's good," the tape said. "Now take a deep breath. And another."

"Whose idea was this?" I muttered, gathering my underwear off the drying rack and putting it the drawer.

"Fine." the tape said, "Now repeat after me, I *love* myself."

"Okay." I told myself, "This was my idea and I can do this." So I repeated after T.J., "I *love* myself."

"I am a *good* person."

"I am basically good," I thought, rolling up a pair of socks. "I am a good person."

"My life is rich and I am blessed."

"Don't push it, T.J.," I thought. But I *said*, "My life is rich and I am blessed."

"I have a loving and forgiving heart."

"I have a loving and forgiving heart," I grumbled, rolling up more socks.

"I love and forgive my ex-girlfriend."

"I love and forgive my ex-girlfriend," I said, choking on my words.

"Except for that incident last winter."

"Except for that incident last winter..." Hey, how'd she know about that?

"I'm still pretty ticked off about that."

Damn right. "I *am* still ticked about that."

"In fact, just thinking about it makes me pretty angry."

"*Very* angry." I told the cassette deck.

"In fact, I feel like picking up a soft object and throwing it across the room."

My hand reached out for the alarm clock.

"A soft object," the tape said. "Like a pillow."

I grabbed Ruby, a stuffed red dinosaur that my ex-lover had given me.

"Don't throw that cute dinosaur," the voice said.

"Fine, I'll throw a pair of rolled-up socks."

"How about a sock?" the voice said.

"I'm ahead of you," I told the tape.

"Well then, throw that object."

I heaved the blue and white socks across the room. My cat flew off the bed and ran for the closet, knocking over the drying rack in the process. Clothes spilled to the floor.

"I am really angry," the tape said.

"I am really angry," I said, throwing another pair, pink this time. The socks hit my change dish and coins flew all over.

"Damn, am I pissed off," the tape said.

"Damn, am I pissed off!" I yelled, flinging yet another pair, these teal.

"I can't believe you bought trendy teal socks," the tape said, "Don't you know they'll be out of style in six months?"

"Shut up!" I screamed, hurling a pair of heavy woolen camping socks directly at the tape player, knocking it over.

"That's good!" the voice said from the floor where the player had landed. "Vent that anger! Beat on a pillow! Let's hear a primal scream!"

"Arrgh!" I yelled, shredding a pillow with my bare hands, feathers flying wildly about.

Suddenly it was quiet. I looked around me. Clothes were strewn everywhere. Nickels and dimes covered the rug. Posters, hit by socks, hung askew. Feathers continued to float down slowly.

I looked at the tape player. Side one was over. I flipped the tape and read the title of side two: *Cleaning up the emotional mess of a break up.* I put it in and pressed PLAY.

FEAR AND READING AT THE YMCA CAMP

A few months ago, in a bold attempt to defy my increasingly reclusive nature, I joined a lesbian reading group. The first few meetings were fine, but then in December one of the women mentioned that the annual "read away" was fast approaching.

I was seized with terror.

Oh sure, at first mention the read away sounds like a harmless enough event: a dozen women sharing a large cabin at the YMCA camp, reading books all weekend. Ah, but you don't know these women. These women are intellectuals, scholars, part of the literati. Most have long strings of initials after their names. But more than that, they are *really into books*.

These women are the kind of people who'll refinish their basements just to build more bookshelves in them. They have a special "book purchase" category in their monthly budgets. If a mugger threatened them with the line, "your books or your life," they'd need a moment to think about it.

Needless to say, I was a tad bit intimidated. Could I keep up as they held a spirited discussion on the relative contributions of the Brontë sisters? I imagined them up well past midnight, expounding the philosophies of Gertrude Stein or debating the place of Joyce Carol Oates in contemporary literature. As a break, I bet they breezed through Colette in the original French.

Before I could weasel my way out of the retreat, the coordinator signed me up for the Saturday night dinner crew.

"At least they take time to eat," I thought, "Maybe I can sneak out of discussions by volunteering to do the dishes."

When the appointed day arrived, I had the best of intentions of getting there on time, lest I walk into the middle of a lunch hour examination of *Sister Outsider* and find myself completely lost. However, procrastination got the best of me and I arrived an hour late.

As it turned out, I'd arrived just after the retreat coordinators opened up the cabin. No one else was around. So much for the myth of the compulsively punctual bibliophile.

Over the next two hours, women slowly filtered in, gathering in the living room. Someone brought out chips and salsa. Homemade cookies were passed around. Everyone acted like normal people: talking about work, politics, kids. I began to relax.

Then Elizabeth, a university professor and avid reader, turned to Justine, a clay sculptor, and asked, "So what books have you read lately?"

"This is it!" I cried to myself, "the moment of truth." I knew Elizabeth would ask me next. Had I read any books besides the book group selection for that month? Would a book count if I'd read it over six weeks ago? I munched hard on my cookie and eyed Justine.

Clearly, she wasn't fazed. "I've been reading a book on my income taxes. Does that count?" she laughed, dipping a blue corn chip in the salsa.

I froze. My god, she'd made the biggest faux pas imaginable. To mention the banality of money here, even jokingly. What would Elizabeth do?

Elizabeth laughed. Laughed? They went on to talk about deductions, while I sat there, slack-jawed. Then Justine asked Elizabeth what *she'd* been reading.

"Oh, I just finished *Scarlett*," she said.

No. Not possible. *Scarlett*? As in the highly touted, miserably written sequel to *Gone With the Wind*?

"You're joking," I said.

"Oh, no," she answered, amused. "My aunt sent it to me for Christmas. The writing's atrocious but it has lots of plot. I love plot."

After that I loosened up. I discovered what "read aways" are really about: 1) Eating. 2) Gossiping. 3) Playing board games. 4) More eating. 5) Taking long walks. 6) Reading.

In that order.

Where I expected to be surrounded by the works of Eudora Welty or Gloria Anzaldúa, I was instead surrounded by lasagna and Cornish game hens. Copies of *Time* Magazine and a Calvin and Hobbes collection lay unashamedly in the living room. Instead of debating *Diving Into The Wreck* or *Woman Warrior*, we played Pictionary and Scrabble.

Someone brought up a copy of Gay Trivia (no, it was not one of the games supplied by the Y camp). More accurately named Gay White Male Trivia, the answers to its questions continually seemed to be Errol Flynn, Judy Garland or "he was killed by an art-deco dildo." I thought we should develop our own version, so we started making up questions, the answers to which continually seemed to be Ma Rainey, the Red Stockings, or "she was Rita Mae Brown's lover."

Of course there were slightly more erudite activities. We debated the European canon, argued about Sonia Johnson's relationship book, even read aloud an Anne Beattie short story.

We also read aloud a satirical lesbian Gothic romance play, in which I was the evil sister next door, who not only turns out to be a lesbian, but was also the one who cut the brake line on the murdered woman's car. Pretty high drama for the Y camp.

The remaining question is, of course, will I be back next year? You bet. And this time I'll bring a murder mystery, cartoon books, and my collection of wind-up toys.

After all, the read away is no place to be serious.

EVERYTHING I NEVER WANTED TO KNOW

While *some* people may have learned everything they needed to know about life in kindergarten, everything I *never* wanted to know about life I learned in Corporate America. But, after being a corporate entity at NBI for the last year and a half, I decided last month to give notice and seek my fortune elsewhere. Fortunately, I took careful notes on my experiences, which I now gladly share with you.

Great Revelation #1. *It never feels like home.* A few weeks after signing up for the ol' 40 hours a week, I realized that the better part of my waking life was going to be spent in a small office with permanently sealed windows. To counteract this gloomy prospect, I brought in an old boom box and three boxes of tapes, a bunch of photographs, a poster of Rosie the Riveter, a 10 x 12 glossy of k. d. lang and an assortment of rocks and shells.

Unfortunately, my two PCs still dominated the scene, so I then trucked in my collection of wind-up toys, a plastic trumpet, three double-faced monster finger puppets, a signed Tuck and Patti photo and my *Dykes to Watch Out For* calendar. Even with all that stuff, it never felt like home. And I guess that's the point. Work in a corporate setting is just that: work. The outer trappings only make it more bearable.

Great Revelation #2. *If you're not feeling like an activist within the queer community, go work for a big company.* My co-workers had so little political consciousness that they thought "social change" meant rescheduling a dinner date. The simple act of posting a Pride Day flyer over my desk caused the entire engineering department to view me as a bona fide militant homosexual. Although I've never participated in civil disobedience, never wheat-pasted flyers in the dead of night, nor even smooched at a kiss-in, I was still bestowed this great honor.

Of course, being a "radical" at NBI had its drawbacks. For instance, a man from telesales caught wind of my new-found status, then cornered me in the lunch room for his "Bill Clinton for President" spiel.

"His wife is terrific," he said, "You'd like her."

"Then why doesn't *she* run?" I asked.

Baffled at my inquiry, he stumbled into another round of rhetoric.

Also foisted upon me was the "feminism is dead because Gloria Steinem wrote a book about self-esteem" topic. To avoid such confrontations, I usually ate lunch in my office. Better to risk a technical writing question than to be forced to defend the feminist movement between bites.

Therefore, my **third Great Revelation** is. . .

Stay out of the lunch room. And not just because of dumb questions. You see, our lunch room mysteriously brings out the worst in women.

Now the women I describe have high-level jobs—reviewing international contracts, interviewing applicants, producing payroll. Clearly they are intelligent people. Then why, I ask the great goddess, do they mutate into such idiots once they congregate for lunch? Apparently, strange forces overpower them, rendering them incapable of talking about anything except dieting. As their "Lite 'n Healthy Entrees" defrost in the microwave, they debate grams of fat, calories per serving, and saturated vs.

unsaturated oils with a fervor I've seen matched only by men reeling off football statistics. Far be it from me to pass judgment upon my sisters, but maybe the calorie counters should read what Gloria has to say about self-esteem.

While the lunch room may not be a hotbed of progressive thought, generally speaking, NBI is a "tolerant" place. Oh, true, someone tore my Coming Out Week flyers off the employee bulletin board. And true, the CEO supported this action by converting the employee bulletin board to an NBI business-only space (nothing like avoiding the issue). But other than that minor attack on my freedom of speech, I was strongly supported in my daily dykedom, especially by those I worked with most closely. This was a good thing because...

Great Revelation #4. *Your office mate knows your life story.* It's fairly unavoidable, especially if you rely on the phone for basic communication. Early on, I gave up trying to maintain any semblance of privacy and accepted that my conversations could be overheard. As my office mate became familiar with the intimate details of my life, I came to rely upon her as a sounding board, as a co-conspirator in the absurdities of corporate bureaucracy and as an on-the-spot therapist. This woman knows more about my family issues, eating habits, buying patterns, therapy sessions and basic fears, hopes and dreams than any one else I know. Good thing we are friends.

The Fifth (and Final) Great Revelation: *Life continues.* So, I've stepped out of the fluorescent world of NBI, back into the searing daylight of self-employment. While I work part-time at a small college, the rest of my life belongs to the unknown. I'm *supposed* to be typesetting my book (a collection of these essays) and by the time you read this column that project should complete. Will this happen? Or will I succumb to the endless task of clearing out my filing cabinet, watching Star Trek reruns and wrestling with inflatable mattresses? Catch me next month for the answer.

THE AMAZING TALE OF
THE INFLATABLE AIR MATTRESS

Last month, I alluded to my recent and colorful exploits with an air mattress. Having received a flood of mail calling for details on this fascinating topic, I now present "The Tale of the Inflatable Air Mattress." (Okay, there *was* no flood of mail. But I needed a lead-in.)

Anyway, back in March, before leaving the world of big business and regular paychecks, I mail-ordered an inflatable mattress. A week later, I came home from a hard day's work (okay, an easy day of freelancing) and lo and behold, there on my steps was a heavy cardboard box.

"My air mattress!" I exclaimed, although I didn't *really* "exclaim." I merely thought it in my head. (I am trying to cut down on talking to myself. It confuses my friends.)

Since I wanted to see if the mattress worked before I (or a house guest) relied on it for a good night's sleep, I decided to inflate it then and there. I cleared some space and spread the mattress out—the pungent yet comforting smell of fresh plastic filling the room. (I'm not kidding about the comforting part. Maybe it reminds me of baby cribs.)

The instructions suggested using a blow dryer to inflate the thing (it's a "full" and you'd likely keel over and pass out if you tried blowing it up on your own) so I dug deep in the attic and found one. I took the dryer into the living room and turned it on, its nozzle pushed against the mattress valve. Air noisily flowed inward. Not a whole lot was happening, though. I waited.

In a corner I saw a crease move ever so slightly. I continued to wait. The middle of the mattress seemed to have expanded, just a touch. Or was I imagining things? Again I tried to be patient. I took deep breaths. I meditated. In. Out. Feel your breath. Let go of control. One with the Universe. Just as blue

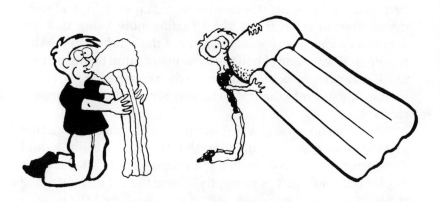

light appeared and I saw the face of the Creator through the purple mists of time—BLAM! the blow dryer sparked and crackled and died. The air mattress sagged despondently.

Fully back in the present, I remained undaunted by this setback. The instructions also said you could use a vacuum cleaner to inflate the mattress. Even though I'd never used a vacuum in reverse, I was up to the challenge. My cat Amanda, on the other hand, upon seeing the vacuum emerge, fled—as is her routine—to far reaches under the bed.

Now, a word about my Kirby vacuum cleaner, a household machinery wonder. A friend gave it to me on my 28th birthday and although it didn't come with a birth certificate, I expect it's about as old as I am. This vacuum has an exterior design not unlike that of a '55 Chevy and it weighs about the same. Its manual lists the unlimited possibilities of this man-made marvel, including an optional Swedish massage unit and knife sharpener. (This part is true!)

With capabilities such as these, I knew that reversing the hoses would be a piece of cake. I removed the vacuum bag, adjusted the new attachments and pressed the "on" switch.

Whoosh! Decades-old dust hurled out of the vacuum, flying around the room. In shock, I flailed about until I finally hit the "off" switch. I looked at the newly created layer of dirt and wondered how to clean it up, the situation now being that the vacuum cleaner was the *source* and not the solution to my dirt problem. Fortunately, I had the presence of mind to unearth my Dustbuster and revacuum the area. I then dumped the dirt from the Dustbuster into the trash can and returned to the vacuum cleaner.

This time, however, I was ready for it. I cunningly placed the end of the vacuum hose in the trash can, so that the dirt would blow directly into it. Whoosh! The air zoomed right into the trash as planned and—just as promptly—blew the old dirt out of the trash. As large, flamboyant swirls of dust circled the room, I once again I fumbled for the "off" switch, then picked up the Dustbuster to clean up the damage.

By now the dirt in the vacuum had been blown clear, so on my third try I hooked up the hose to the air mattress and let it fill. This time there was no need for patience or steady breathing nor was there the slightest opportunity to see purple mist, let alone the face of the Creator. No ma'am! *This time* the mattress had a life of its own, swelling up and flinging itself about my living room. In its exuberance, it knocked over the scratching post, shoved a stereo speaker up against the wall and even threatened to topple the couch. I scurried around, moving magazine baskets and wobbly lamps to higher ground. When the mattress looked firm, I turned the vacuum off and sealed the opening.

Exhausted from the last hour's antics, I dropped onto the mattress. Amanda emerged from the bedroom and eyed the mattress with an expression that said, "A horizontal scratching post?" Before she could bare a single claw, I grabbed her and placed her on my stomach. "Don't even think about it," I told her, "don't even think about it."

NO STAMP OF APPROVAL

Some people are content to just lick and stick, but *I* take my postage stamps seriously. Uncle Sam can't fool me—I know that stamps are yet one more insidious form of government influence.

Don't believe it? Take another look. Notice how it's always men on stamps. Oh, sure there's an occasional woman, just like the single African American who's honored for Black History month. But basically it boils down to my "you gotta be a dead guy" theory; that is, you have to be a deceased male before they'll put your face on a stamp.

Goddess forbid the U.S. government should honor someone while they're still around to appreciate it. The end product of this practice is stamps bearing the likeness of safe, conservative people whose radical fire, if they ever had any, is banished, quashed and cancelled. When Martin Luther King appears on a stamp is there any mention of his protest against the Viet Nam War? Would mainstream America lick a Cole Porter stamp if they knew the man was gay?

But I digress. I was talking about women on stamps and how there aren't any. Oh, *occasionally* we show up, but notice how we are continually relegated to the odd 23¢ or 4¢ stamps, along with the "modes of transportation" series. That's right—outstanding women like Rachel Carson get lumped with stamps honoring Tractor Trailers and Steam Carriages.

Let's face it, the only way for a woman to consistently be on a first-class postage stamp is for her name to be Madonna. And I don't mean Madonna the performer, I mean Madonna as in Jesus's mom. What? Have you already forgotten the "you've got to be dead" rule?

But I understand how you could forget. I forgot the other day, too. I'd heard that the post office had issued a series of stamps honoring comedians. I rushed down there, expecting to see Lily Tomlin, Whoopi Goldberg or Marga Gomez smiling up at me from those tiny squares of paper. Instead I got dead males: Jack Benny, Laurel and Hardy, Bergen and McCarthy. And of course, one token female, Fanny Brice.

Needless to say, I was not impressed.

Several years ago I thought perhaps the post office had just run out of good ideas for stamps. In order to help them out, I grabbed one of those handy complaint/suggestion forms that the post office kindly provides and dashed off some ideas.

"Dear Mr. Postmaster General," I wrote, "how about a stamp honoring single mothers raising kids without child support? How about celebrating organic foods? How about commending social workers who are paid ungodly small salaries while the government continues to fund the military industrial complex?" You know, I never did hear back from the General. (I wonder if he's part of the military industrial complex?)

Since I never saw my suggestions appear on any stamps, I reasoned that the post office actually had a long line up of really important events and people they needed to honor and they just hadn't gotten around to my request yet. But as the months rolled by and I continued to see what *did* get on stamps—CIA officers, dead white movie actors and the thrilling hobby of Numismatics (what's going on here? Is the post office in cahoots with the

Mint?), I grew increasingly disillusioned with the process.

And of course, who can forget the whole Elvis issue? Let's ignore the national debt, eroding civil rights, increased acts of domestic violence—what's really important here is do we want the young Elvis or the old Elvis on our postage stamps. Oh yes, let's gear up for a national vote on the question.

Can you imagine them doing that with, for instance, a Holly Near stamp? Attention Americans, cast your vote for either a) the short-haired Holly Near in her "Imagine My Surprise" period or b) the recent bisexual Holly Near, with her softer, more "femme" look.

Concerning the Elvis controversy, though, one thing at least is settled: if the Postal Service is putting his image on a stamp, then Elvis must be dead.

The final blow to my "equality on postage stamps" campaign came when they devoted a whole series to fishing flies. That's right, fishing flies! They can't give a single stamp over to honoring feminism or recognizing the gay and lesbian rights struggle, but they can devote five whole stamps to fish bait with ludicrous names such as Jock Scott, Royal Wulff and Muddler Minnow. (Come to think of it, "Jock Scott" sounds like a gay male video star and "Royal Wulff" *does* conjure up images of a drag queen. Nonetheless, that doesn't score any points for gay rights.)

So what's a progressive-minded feminist to do? I say it's time to print our own stamps! If we wait for the post office to take action, it will be the 22nd Century before we start pasting "Reproductive Freedom" or Pat Parker stamps on our letters. Frankly I'm not that patient. So get out your markers, your colored pencils, your color laser printers and let those creative juices flow. And if anyone objects, just tell them that a stamp honoring "creative expression" is long overdue.

A WORD ABOUT WRITING

Once upon a time, I believed that if I limited my donations to only lesbian and gay groups, I'd only have to contend with an occasional request for money. I honestly thought there were only a few queer non-profits around. . . until I wrote that first innocent check. Then wham-o! Suddenly I'm on the SuperList, and every homo cause in the world has my name and address.

Some, like the Human Rights Campaign Fund are very upscale, with $150-a-plate fundraisers. Others, like PROJECT 10 (focusing on gay and lesbian youth) are down-to-earth in their approach. I've gotten requests to subscribe to Gay Community News (I did), buy books from Firebrand (I will), donate to a straight but supportive congressman (I didn't).

But my all-time favorite mailing came a few weeks ago. It was from the magazine OUT/LOOK and it started out like this: (The comments in parenthesis are mine.)

Writers and artists are absolutely central to the lives of the lesbian and gay community. (Being a writer myself, I had to agree.)

What would we do without their artistic contributions. . .? (Probably surrender ourselves to network sitcoms, then slowly wither away from ennui.)

And yet their creative minds face daunting challenges. Their talents go unrecognized and they cannot make their living through their work. (Isn't that the truth!)

So far, I really liked this letter. It was. . . validating. I read on.

Two years ago the OUT/LOOK Foundation established the Writer's and Artist's Fund. . .

"This is it!" I thought. "I've been discovered! OUT/LOOK wants to give me a $10,000 grant to finish those three half-written novels!"

Then I read the next paragraph.

Won't you support the Writer's and Artist's Fund with a tax-deductible donation?

Oh. Like everyone else, they wanted my money.

But that letter got me thinking. It's not true that queers can't make money through their writing. Perhaps all those struggling artists just don't know the tricks. So for them, I present *Ellen's Informal Guide to Making Money with Your Writing.*

1. Write trash. That's right, start spewing garbage. Fiction, nonfiction—either's okay. If nonfiction is your choice, write loaded innuendo about Oprah, John Kennedy or Nancy Reagan. Kitty Kelly and Geraldo Rivera's love triangle with Governor Pete Wilson would also be a fine subject.

2. Write a sequel to *Gone with the Wind.* Yes, sequels can certainly bring in the green stuff. So, if you have no problem with personal morals, this kind of writing may be for you.

3. Write romance. Easier than researching unauthorized biographies or finding an established best seller to rip off, writing romance novels can be a great little money-maker. Yes, you too can earn a fortune writing books entitled *Beneath the Quivering Elm, Beyond the Quaking Aspens* (quivering and quaking are essential elements in romance), or *Far, Far Away from Respectable Literature.*

Of course, almost all of the thousands of romance novels out there are written by the same twelve authors. They just work under a variety of *nom de plume's*—Monique LaRavish, Belle

Noir, etc. So it might be tough to break into the field. And, of course, you'll have to change your name.

NOTE: To make money at this, you must get your genders right. Follow the example below.

Correct: *Her secret place ached with desire as she watched Benjamin's chest muscles ripple.*

Incorrect: *Her secret place ached with desire as she watched Linda's chest muscles ripple.*

While you *can* make money writing lesbian romance, your profit will be between 2% and 0% of what het romances bring in. Maybe less.

5. Write about writing. A great fall-back trick. Aspiring authors always have a dozen "how to write" books lined up in their bookcases—*Write On, Write Away, Writing Your Heart Out.* These books usually have long subtitles like, *How to Transform Your Life (and Get Rich) with a No. 2 Pencil.* Oddly enough, authors in this genre rarely have had a real book or article published.

6. Be brilliant. If you are a genius like, for instance, Amy Tan, Margaret Atwood or Paule Marshall, *and* you have a good agent *and* you get several breaks *and* you work your butt off, then yes, you can make money writing real literature. Once again, however, immensely talented authors such as these don't make nearly as much as do the trash writers. And, as always, you'll have better luck with the bucks if you don't bring homosexuality onto the page.

7. Write anyway. Okay, so the above suggestions are rather discouraging. But write anyway. Write poems or novels or essays or investigative articles or even romances, but be sure to bring in those queer characters and themes. Join a writer's group and get constructive feedback; send your work to lesbian, bi and gay publications. And remember, when we buy our own books, we support our own culture. And, hey, if you've got any cash left over, you can always send a few bucks to OUT/LOOK.

FINDING A THERAPIST
(THE REAL, TRUE STORY)

We've all seen them: those ominous "how-to-find-a-therapist" articles. How to locate, screen and interview. What to ask about education, homophobia, insurance, fees. By following these articles' recommendations, you'll (supposedly) build a trusting, nurturing, non-codependent relationship with the therapist of your choice. My reply to such well-meaning treatises? "Let's get serious, shall we?"

Finding a therapist is *never* a logical progression of steps. Why? Because 97.2% of all lesbians wait until they're absolutely desperate before seeking professional help. But I won't bore you with statistics. Instead, I'll regale you with my own real, true story of seeking couples counseling.

About a year ago, Lori and I conceded that our relationship didn't stand an ice cube's chance in hell if we didn't get some counseling and fast. We each had our own therapist, but needed someone new and objective. We figured, where better to get a referral than from another therapist? So we started calling.

I began by phoning my friend Ronnie and asking her for recommendations.

"Millie Goulash is real good," she said.

"That won't work. Millie and Lori are friends. In fact, Lori's getting referrals from Millie right now."

"Oh. How about Jamie Cavanaugh?"

"Nah, I walk her dogs once a week."

"Amy Kroger?"

"Uh, uh. We worked on the March on Washington together."

"Joanie, the Hakomi therapist?"

"A close friend of mine goes to her. Could be messy."

Eventually, Ronnie came up with names I could use and later that evening, Lori and I compared lists.

"Millie suggested Ronnie," Lori told me, " and of course, my own therapist."

"Ronnie suggested Mattie Horn."

"Is she at the Mental Health Center?"

"Yeah."

"Anyone at the Center is out. I might have an internship there in the fall—conflict of interest. How about Raenna Pernoff?"

"Nope, she was a graphics client of mine. Cicily Chung?"

"Uh, uh. She's adjunct faculty at school. I could have her as an instructor next year."

Left with precious few choices, we called other therapists we knew and got more names. After weeding through these, Lori and I came up with seven women with whom we had no personal or professional conflicts. I returned to the phone and called them. It went like this:

"Sorry, I don't do couples counseling."

"I've closed my private practice."

"I charge $110 for a 50-minute session. Is that okay?"

"I've got a slot opening in six weeks." Pause on my part. She continued. "Let me guess. No way you two will last another six days, let alone six weeks without counseling. Am I right?"

At least she had a sense of humor.

Finally, we found two therapists we could interview. Now a word about the initial visit: it is a nightmare. Here you are, dog-tired from constant fighting or deafening silence and the two of you—together—are supposed to make an intelligent decision as to where to drop four hundred bucks in the next six weeks.

It's best to arrive prepared—with written notes if possible. This way your mind can remain objective while your heart watches your dreams vanish as quickly as the ozone layer. First off, you must ascertain each therapist's modus operandi: i.e., what kind of therapy does she practice? This is relatively easy.

If her office has a leather couch, tall book shelves with imposing tomes and a large, orderly desk: she's a clinical psychologist. If she has wicker furniture, lots of plants and a window with a decent view, she's a feminist therapist.

If she has sparse furniture, asymmetrical flower arrangements and framed Tibetan calligraphy on the wall, she's a contemplative Buddhist psychologist. If there's no furniture (though plenty of pillows) plus incense and stuffed animals, she's an anti-traditional lesbian therapist with a sliding fee.

Pretty simple, huh?

Anyway, back to Lori and me. As I'd said, we'd come up with two candidates: one she liked and one I liked. After one session with each, I liked the one she'd suggested (abundant ferns and wicker furniture) and she liked the one I'd suggested (imposing tomes in bookcase). After further discussion, "abundant ferns" won out, but after another session with her, we decided she had fuzzy boundaries and we were back to square one.

At this point, we considered the large sum of money we'd set aside for therapy and decided that if we were going to break up (and we certainly were heading in that direction) we might as well go out in style. So, we booked three nights at the Ruby Slipper in Taos and wined, dined and hot-tubbed our way through a wonderful vacation. Needless to say, the magic returned and we lived happily ever after.

The End

Author's Note: Okay. I embellished the ending a bit. Well, *all right*; I lied. We never went to Taos, and as everyone knows, Lori and I broke up. However, I staunchly believe in poetic license, a literary term meaning "writers can make up whatever facts they want."

But the honest truth is, Lori and I are enjoying each other's company, now that we're out of the relationship. So, in all truthfulness, the magic *has* returned, and we're both living happily ever after.

The End (Really)

TRUTH, JUSTICE AND THE LESBIAN WAY

Faster than a speeding Harley. . .
More powerful than a leather-clad butch. . .
Able to leap tall homophobes in a single bound. . .

Look! Up in the air! It's a bird! It's a plane! It's Super Dyke!
Super Dyke.

Man, the things I would do if I were Super Dyke. First of all,
I wouldn't say "man." I'd say "goddess" and not feel self-
conscious about it.

If I were Super Dyke and a co-worker told a "faggot" joke, I
wouldn't bury my head in my hands (as I'm tempted to do) and
mumble to myself, "I gotta get another job." Nor would I settle
for meekly saying (as I generally do), "I don't appreciate that
kind of humor."

Hell, no! If I were Super Dyke, I'd jump up from my chair,
leap onto the table and rip open my shirt, exposing my deep
lavender Super Dyke suit, complete with tights, cape, and a hot
pink "D" emblazoned across the chest.

"I am Super Dyke," I'd tell the joker, "and I will not stand for
such bigotry. Not only does it spread hate and ignorance, but

such outright stupidity is an embarrassment to all of us who work with you." If that didn't shut him up, I'd turn his ears purple.

Of course, if I were Super Dyke I wouldn't be in a corporate job. I'd work for a non-profit agency that educated women about breast cancer, or investigated toxic waste dumping, or provided legal defense for lesbians in child custody cases. Maybe all three.

If I were Super Dyke, I'd march with Queer Nation, protest with ACT-UP, be on the speaker's bureau for P-FLAG. I'd belong to dozens of lesbian and gay organizations—NGLTF, LHA, MCC, GMHC, HRCF—*and* I'd know what all the initials stood for.

Basically, if I were Super Dyke, I wouldn't put up with so much crap from rich white guys. I'd walk right up to the owners of the all the big hotels in town, look them right in the eye and say, "You make this hotel accessible for people using wheelchairs or I'll kill you."

I'd fly over "Operation Rescue" and drop bags of ripe compost on their heads. I'd make Cardinal Cook tithe his annual salary to Planned Parenthood. I'd swoop down on CU football Coach McCartney, grab him, then drop him off in the middle of the roughest dyke leather bar I could find.

Yup, if I were Super Dyke, no gay-bashers, anti-Semites or racists would dare cross *my* path. Educators and religious leaders, however, would seek me out for advice and consultation, which I would give freely. Yes, I would do this in addition to my full-time job at the non-profit agency, my weekly volunteer work with gay youth, my two-nights-a-week of anti-homophobia training classes and my every-other-Thursday-evening Eco-feminism reading group.

You see, if I were Super Dyke, I'd have my personal shit together too. I'd overcome my white, upper-middle-class anxiety and live in a racially mixed, economically diverse neighborhood with people of all ages. We'd have community meetings where we'd process our racist, classist, ageist, ableist, sizeist and heterosexist issues. On the weekends we'd work together in our community garden.

If I were Super Dyke, I'd bike to work, eat organic food, write to my elected officials and buy books from small publishing houses. I'd learn Spanish, Hmong and American Sign Language, dialog with my bisexual friends, reclaim my Judaism. I'd mediate, do T'ai Chi, go to full-moon chants and, unless I received inner guidance to speak, I'd sit in quiet contemplation at Quaker meetings.

If I were Super Dyke, I'd know my Mary Daly, Sonia Johnson and Audre Lorde inside out. I'd subscribe to OUT/LOOK, OutWeek and BlackOut, and I'd make time to read them all.

If I were Super Dyke, I'd boycott Coca-Cola, Burroughs-Wellcome and Domino's Pizza. I wouldn't drink Coors beer, El Salvadorean coffee or Nestle's Quik, but I wouldn't go around feeling morally superior to those who did. (Not outwardly, at least.)

I'd avoid anything plastic.

Yeah, if I were Super Dyke, I'd be outgoing yet inward-seeking, assertive yet sensitive, intellectual yet funny. I would always return my phone messages, write to my great-aunt monthly, grow my own herbs, recycle my paper bags, eat up the leftovers before they grew mold, change the cat box more often and of, course, make wild, passionate, artful and tender love with my devoted partner of fourteen years.

Yes, if *I* were Super Dyke... I'd probably give myself a heart attack.

So maybe I don't need to be Super Dyke. Maybe I don't have to do everything. Maybe instead of Super Dyke, I could be Pretty-Good Dyke, starting out with a handful of these things and move up slowly. With forethought, with sincerity, with dedication.

And maybe that is super enough all by itself.

A FINAL THANK YOU

Ooh, the acknowledgments page.
This is where the author gets to name drop, right?
Yeah. We can see if she's friends with any famous queer people.
If you read between the lines, you might pick up on her current lover.
That's how we found out that Margie Adam was lovers with—
Yeah, that's right.
Of course, she might just list her friends. People nobody's heard of.
Boring!
Hey, if you wrote a book, would you thank me in print?
Maybe. . .

Some are famous, some are local heroes and all have been important to me in my writing life.

To Rosalind Warren—a wonderful writer, brilliant editor and funny human being. Her publication of my work in *Women's Glib* started me on my way. Thanks to Jewelle Gomez and Alison Bechdel for their warmth and inspiration. To Kate Clinton, Marga Gomez, Jane Wagner and Karen Williams for being brilliant.

Thanks to Noreen Stevens for her wonderful illustrations and imagination. And to Lori and Jan, for their editing and proofreading skills. Any remaining errors are those of the author (me), who kept making changes up until the very last minute. My appreciation also goes to the Boulder Queer Collective and the Boulder City Council who helped finance this book with generous grants.

Thanks to my family and relatives—strong role models in my childhood and great fans today. And to Sash, April, Jamie, Carol, Verna, Robin, Patty, Lori, Martha, Cyn, Kathryn, Mickey, Kat, Eladia, Jabe, Patty, Jim, Sue, Christopher, Karin, Holly, Rebekah, Michelle, Katya and Zeke—friends who I wanted to mention individually, but whose names I had to list carefully so that ex-lovers didn't appear next to each other in print. And to everyone with whom I've processed feelings, vented anger, hashed through politics or conducted a conflicted relationship. Or otherwise loved.

And finally, thanks to everyone who's ever written me a letter, stopped me at a Pride Parade, or sought me out at a softball game just to say, "Hey, I like your writing. I think you're funny."

ABOUT THE AUTHOR

Once you've read this book, you'll know quite a lot about the author, except perhaps, what she looked like when she was sixteen months old. So here's a picture of the author and her mom at the Jersey shore, where she spent many happy summers building sand castles. Currently, Ellen lives in landlocked Colorado with her inner child, her cat and her cat's inner kitten, all of whom have yet to contribute to the rent.

ABOUT THE ILLUSTRATOR

Noreen Stevens is a comic artist and gay/lesbian activist living in Winnipeg, Manitoba, Canada. She derives special pleasure, through her art, in causing homophobes to jump up and down, pull on their hair and say, "You can't do that, you can't do that," when in fact they have already been proven wrong. Her offering to the rest of the world is the joy, celebration and catharsis of laughter.

If you enjoyed *Can't Keep A Straight Face*, you'll probably get a kick out of these humor books edited by Roz Warren:

Women's Glib: A Collection of Women's Humor. Cartoons, stories and poems by America's funniest women wits that will knock you of your chair laughing. Alison Bechdel, Nicole Hollander, Julie Blackwoman, Roz Chast, Noreen Stevens and more.

Women's Glibber: State of the Art Women's Humor. Madonna! Sex! Poultry! and much more. 300 pages of laughs from women humorists the world over, including Molly Ivins, Jane Wagner, June Jordan, Nina Paley and Lynda Barry.

Kitty Libber: Cat Cartoons by Women: Hilarious feline funnies by all the best women cartoonists.

As always, please support your local feminist/lesbian/progressive bookstore when ever possible. To order these books by mail, use the coupon below.

And if you're a true connoisseur of women's humor, you won't want to miss these Laugh Lines' publications.

Can't Keep A Straight Face: A Lesbian Looks and Laughs at Life: Ellen Orleans; Essays about self-improvement, softball, the religious right, coming out, breaking up, saving the earth and much more!

Weenie-Toons: Women Cartoonists Mock Cocks: If you've ever laughed at a penis, this is the book for you!